DRIVEN
to
CHANGE

Jeff Heiser

NEWMAN SPRINGS PUBLISHING
320 Broad Street
Red Bank, NJ 07701

First originally published by Newman Springs Publishing 2019

ISBN 978-1-64531-249-9 (Paperback)
ISBN 978-1-64531-250-5 (Digital)

Printed in the United States of America

Contents

Acknowledgments 5

In the Beginning 9

My Why...16

    Family 18

    Living with Guilt 20

Getting Started..22

    Your Story, Your Journey 22

    Define Your own Relationships.................................28

    Purpose Driven 37

    The Man in the Mirror 39

    Disliked? Who Cares! 46

    The Orange Peel Effect: Peeling Back Your Layers 48

Developing Personal Character..50

    Winning Is Contagious 50

    The Importance of Setting Priorities........................55

    Are You Living a Lie?..62

    Your Authentic Signature 64

    Stop Complaining! Be Thankful Every Day................73

    Attitude Is Everything 74

    Living Well..81

Controlling Your Anger..94

    External Stimuli that Generates Anger......................94

    Different Ways to Express Anger 98

    Anger Management...101

    What We Say Can Hurt 107

Stand Up to Be Counted 110
    Positive Self-Image 113
    Your Personal Character 116
    Commitment 120
    Hard Work 125
Choices You Make 129
How You Think 137
    You Become What You Think 142
    Is Fear Holding You Back? 146
    Changing How You Think Is the Difference....................155
    Your Negative Inner Voice 158
    Think Big..161
Mental Toughness 163
    Life Will Be Challenging..163
    Hard Work Is a Turning Point 166
    Motivation 167
    Confidence..169
    Focus...171
    Composure 173
    Resilience 175
    Wrapping Up Mental Toughness 177
Your Next Steps..181
    All Things Are Possible..181
    Nothing Is Guaranteed..182
    Are You Making a Difference? 186
    Possibilities...188
    Stop Taking Criticism So Personally 189
    A Word about Your Online Relationships........................190
    Stop Being Sick and Tired of Not Knowing What
        You Want from Life..191
    Anyone Can Realize Success 193
    Appreciate Life 195

Acknowledgments

To April—my wife, my best friend and my partner in this crazy life.

April, you have taught me more about life and myself than anyone else on this planet. You have been my encourager, my supporter, and you are always there when the going gets tough. Through your love and understanding, you have given me more opportunities and second chances than I feel I deserve. Thank you for always believing in me.

A special thank you to Dr. Brian Heiser for the time and energy he gave helping me to find clarity, purpose, and meaning as I wrote this book. Without his help, this book would not have become a reality.

If families are who you love, then it should be clear why families are the most important aspect of my life. Thank you to my family—my son Jeffrey, my daughter Jennifer, my son Brian; their families; my grandchildren, mom, and siblings; my nieces and nephews; and my sister-in-law and her husband for accepting me as I am with all my faults and misgivings. I know at times, it has been hard to live with me. At times, it has been hard for me to live with me. Thank you all for continuing to love me.

It is not the critic who counts; not the man who points out how the strong man stumbles, or where the doer of deeds could have done them better. The credit belongs to the man who is actually in the arena, whose face is marred by dust and sweat and blood; who strives valiantly; who errs, who comes short again and again, because there is no effort without error and shortcoming; but who does actually strive to do the deeds; who knows great enthusiasms, the great devotions; who spends himself in a worthy cause; who at the best knows in the end the triumph of high achievement, and who at the worst, if he fails, at least fails while daring greatly, so that his place shall never be with those cold and timid souls who neither know victory nor defeat.

—Theodore Roosevelt

In the Beginning

Every day that I wake up and put my feet on the floor is a day that I am thankful for receiving the gift of another day. When you live life on purpose, things happen. Things might not happen for you today, but eventually, things change. They especially change when you are intentional about living your life. Back in 1993, I sat in my room; I was by myself and I had to make a choice. I had two options: (1) create a purpose-filled life by making the positive changes I needed to make (2) give up, accept defeat, and end my life. I chose option one. I knew in that moment that the only way this was going to happen was for me to be serious about the necessary changes I needed to make. I had to ask for help. I needed to be committed. These changes were necessary.

At times, what you will read in this book is tough. What you will read is authentic. What you will read may cause you to become angry or upset. What you read will feel as if this book is directed at you. That is okay! My intent is to get your attention in a way that you will understand what it takes to change and build a happy, fulfilled life. This book is for anyone stuck in life. This book is for the person who is floundering like a fish out of water, gasping for air. You may be in a bad place right now, you might be in a very dark place, but trust me when I say this: "If you are reading this book you have taken the first step to changing your life." You might be in a dead-end job that you hate, or you might not even have a job. You might not have the house you want or the luxury vehicle you dreamed about. Your house may be your car as you wander from parking lot to parking lot each night. You might have demons talking in your head, helping you relive a bad experience repeatedly. You may be experiencing overwhelming feelings of loss or anxiety. All these things add up and need to be changed. If you are not deliberate about doing what is necessary to bring change in your life, you will end up living an unfulfilled life.

Success is measured in many ways. For some, success means being filthy rich, where owning a 14k gold toilet that they dreamed about sitting on every morning is a reality. For me, success means that I am here today. I am here today to be able to share my message and journey with you. I will lay out common sense thoughts and ideas on how you can make changes and take the steps that are necessary to become successful in life. I will present ideas on how to step out of your comfort zone that you may be trapped in.

Now is the time to become intentional! Today is the day you take the first step that will change your life forever. There are so many people who just drift through life with little direction. They lack purpose. They have no plan. To live more successfully, you must be willing to take the steps that bring change to your sense of purpose and direction in life. What you do today—that first step toward change—has a direct and profound relationship with how your life will unfold from this point forward. Just as yesterday determined what your today is, today will determine what your tomorrow will become.

When I talk with people about how they view success and what they personally believe success is, I am amazed by the different responses. Some people believe success is all about luck. They believe that successful people put all their chips on red and struck it big. They continue to believe successful people are always in the right place at the right time. They place all their hope and efforts in the belief that someday, their number will be called, and they too will someday be in the right place at the right time.

Other individuals believe success is something magical. Something mystical, like a unicorn or a half-man, half-bull taken right out of a Greek mythology book. They also believe that there must be a secret formula for success. As if there was some shortcut they can take where they hit an "easy" button and all their dreams will come true. These people spend their entire life living in a Disney movie chasing some secret formula while hoping the stars will align just right so they too may follow a rabbit down a mythical hole to Wonderland. These people are constantly looking for shortcuts that are never found—they don't exist.

Then there are the people who believe others are successful because they helped them get there. Do you ever feel like you do so much for others but you never get a piece of the pie? I hope you are not one of the people who wait around for change to happen just to find out you are several numbers short of the winning lottery number. You can do something about it! Stop waiting around for something to happen. It is common knowledge that you have a better chance of getting hit by lightning than winning the lottery. The change is simple. It is all up to you and how intentional you want to be about your life. Where you are heading is directly correlated with the decisions you make. If you want to change, you must become more deliberate about the change you want. If you continue to wait for something, you may be waiting around for a long time as others pass you by.

Do you remember when you were young, every summer your parents would pack all the luggage into the car along with your siblings and you would embark on the great American vacation? As the car slowly ventured down the interstate going ten miles per hour under the speed limit, you would look out the window, waving at the cars as they passed you by. This, metaphorically speaking, is a symbolic view of your journey through life. Sitting, watching as the world around you passes you by as you wait for something to happen. We all know people who have waited their entire life for something to happen, for their number to be called, for their destination to magically appear, to be in the right place at the right time waiting for their moment to happen. All they had to do was become serious about taking that first step for the magic to begin.

Yes, it sounds simple. But if it is that simple, how can it work? It is simple, but it takes hard work. If your life is not where you want it to be, YOU have the power to change it. The beauty of stepping out and trying new things is that you get to see what works and what doesn't. What the experts call it is trial and error. Trying new things will help you figure out what brings change in your life and what doesn't. The more things you try, the more you learn from experience, and the more resilient you become. As you step out of your comfort zone to where the magic happens, the easier it is to learn innovative ideas and concepts that allow you to experience things you could have never imagined. It is simple when you think about it. If you act to experience something new and you fail, your success lies in the fact that you stepped out of your comfort zone in the first place. As the old saying goes, "When you are bucked off the horse, you must get back on." This sentence holds true value. Regardless if you fail, you still had the courage to try in the first place. This initial courage makes you an instant success and a more positive person in the long run.

Once you step out to engage in new ideas, you will notice a momentum change. If you stay focused on expanding and exploring new concepts, you become the proverbial snowball becoming bigger and bigger as you gain momentum down the mountain. As you gain momentum, more positive things will come your way! You must believe this. Let's read this again. AS YOU GAIN MOMENTUM, MORE POSITIVE THINGS WILL COME YOUR WAY! Positive thought is a powerful thing. If you want to have more success in your own life, set your intentions on what you want and stay positive. Create a goal, commit yourself then attack it! Attack it every damn day—not quitting until you reach it. The view from the top and the feeling of achievement is second to none. Big or small, the size of the steps you take to get there do not matter. The fact is you made it! If your steps are in the direction of what you are trying to achieve, you set in motion a new course for your life, and this is a powerful thing.

Success, achievement, winning—heck, call it greatness. I don't care what you call success. The fact is that positive change starts with you believing in yourself. Bottom line: if you don't believe in yourself, no one else will either. Period. You know that feeling you have when someone gives you a compliment? Or when someone attractive catches your eye as you read your book upside down, she then takes it upon herself to call you out on it and all you can do is smile and laugh? Those are all good feelings, right? What if you could feel those good feelings by calling them up at will? We can, but the problem rests in the ability of becoming our own worst enemy. We have voices in our head that talk us right out of things that are good for us. These voices stop us dead in our tracks. Why? Because we lack confidence.

As we grow older, our confidence in achievement and how we convince ourselves to be courageous evolve and dwindle. If our friends were to talk to each other the way the voices in our heads talk to us, we would never stand for it. We would tell them to get lost. Why is it then that we cannot do the same thing for the voices in our head that keep us from stepping outside of our comfort zone? The answer is simple. We are consumed with excuses of why we can't instead of why we can. "I can't do that or achieve this because of X, Y and Z." It is easy to make excuses to keep ourselves safe and sound, bundled up in our blanket of protection in our comfort zone.

When you're pursuing success, excellence is no substitution. I think anyone can achieve excellence if they work hard and continue to practice personal development. Excellence is just being the best at something everyone else does. But success is doing things others only dream about. The problem is most people believe they don't have what it takes. To be frank, some people are meant to be followers, and that is okay. But being a follower is not you, or else you wouldn't be reading this. Many followers don't believe they can be successful. They believe living a fulfilled, successful life is only for others. They convince themselves they are not good enough to lead and achieve real success, so they make excuses and play follow the leader.

What I hear most from others is, "I can't, I don't have a degree, I don't have the money," or "I don't have the time." It seems like there is always time for excuses but never enough time to make the changes people want to make in their lives. Over time, it becomes comfortable and a routine to use excuses and stay put in an imaginary comfort zone. Success does not occur without a change. The change you want does not happen until the excuses stop. However, the silent whisper of excuses inside your head can be stopped by making a simple choice. I learned you must encourage yourself. You must believe in yourself. You must lift yourself up and become your number 1 fan. If you do not encourage and believe in yourself, you do not win.

It is said that if it is important enough to you, you will find a way. If not, you will find an excuse. Excuses serve as distractions that help us avoid achieving our desires. Excuses protect our ego from potential anxiety and shame we might experience if we fail while chasing our desires. The excuses we make keep us from trying. If we don't try, we don't fail. But if you try, you will never lose. You will either win, or you will learn. Using excuses to avoid trying, you are automatically guaranteeing your failure. Excuses enable you to shift the focus from yourself to something less relative. Regardless, excuses do not bring us success. Many argue with me that excuses can change your life by allowing you to feel less anxious, less burdened, and letting you off the hook. My response is always, "What keeps us stuck are the excuses we make."

Most people I speak with have the same excuses why they are stuck in life. I explain to them that "if you want to change your life, you must stop having excuses why you can't change your life." The first step to changing your life is to give up the excuses why you cannot by making the choice to why you can. Make the choice to live life on purpose and stop having excuses why you cannot.

Recently, I spoke at a jail in Baker City, Oregon. After speaking, I had the opportunity to speak one-on-one with a young man that had been incarcerated on various drug charges. I asked him what he thought was the reason for being locked up. He gave me every excuse you can think of, every reason you can imagine, except for one—the most important one. When he was done, I said to him, "What got you locked up is the same thing that will get you out of here." I will never forget his facial expression in response to my statement. I remember, he looked at me like I was crazy. As if I told him, "I just shit my pants." I said to him, "It was a choice you made to break the law, and it will be a choice you make to complete your program that will bring your release from jail. Unless you stick with your choice to successfully complete your rehabilitation program, you will remain incarcerated."

He remained silent for a few moments. As he stared at the floor, I asked him "You okay?" He said, "Yes, sir, I just never heard it put like that. It has made me realize that most of my life, I have made a lot of excuses for the bad choices I've made." In that moment, the young man's life was changed.

Purposeful living is a choice. This is a choice that only you can make. Eric Thomas said that "when you want to succeed as bad as you want to breathe, then you'll be successful." If you are willing to begin living your life intentionally, your life will be uncommon. You will live a life that others only dream of.

My Why

My wife and I were stationed in Puerto Rico in 1977. We were young, in love, and in the Navy. Times were tough, but we were eager to start our life together. After two years of being stationed on the island of Puerto Rico, I met fear face-to-face. I will never forget the moment. I was twenty-two years old in December 1979 when, during the early morning hours, the Navy bus I am usually on was ambushed by terrorists. Two of my friends, John Ball and Emil White, were killed. Ten others were wounded. It was a dreadful day. A day where I can still hear the helicopters roaring overhead as they were landing to pick me up. I can still smell the Marine heroes assigned to put their lives on the line to protect my life. I still have days when I am filled with the anxiety and fear that was etched deep into my mind that December day.

For many years following the event in 1979, the voices in my head persisted. Over time, they became louder, continuously convincing me to refrain from talking about the attack. "Don't talk about that morning, just have a few drinks, you'll be fine." The voices would urge on. "One more drink won't hurt!" After many years of "One more drink won't hurt," I would come to realize the full impact this statement had.

In 1993, my friend took his own life. At his funeral in front of everyone, his wife blamed me and my drinking for his death. I was completely devastated. Sitting, listening to her speak, I became completely numb. I became completely empty inside. The only thing that remained were the voices. They quickly became louder and stronger as the feelings of doubt and selflessness filled my thoughts. These very same voices urged me, as if yelling at me to go home and do the same thing. I will never forget the moment when I sat on the edge of my bed, devastated and full of fear. I had a choice that I needed to make. Could I muster up whatever courage I had left, face my fears, and fix myself, or should I listen to the voices in my head and end the pain? I closed my eyes. Time seemed to stand still. Seconds turned into minutes. Minutes seemed like an eternity. As time passed, I continued to contemplate my decision.

I accepted help. I worked to silence the voices etched deep inside my mind. I quit drinking.

As time passed over many years, I refused to speak about the effects that event in December of '79 had on me. In 2010, I decided it was time to take my first step on stage to speak about the cause and effect the terrorist attack had. This was also the first time that I would tell my wife the story and reveal the fear and struggles I had for so many years. I would be lying to you and myself if I told you this moment was easy. IT WAS HARD! IT WAS UNCOMFORTABLE! As I readied myself to go on stage, I remember looking out from backstage and saw my wife sitting right there in the front row. I had to go back to the dressing room and talk myself off the ledge. I remember looking at myself in the mirror and saying, "YOU CAN DO THIS! YOU CAN DO THIS!" I went on stage. As I walked toward center stage, I found my wife again making eye contact as I told her I loved her. I smiled at her and began telling my story.

I am telling you this because whatever your goals are, at some point, you will have to make a choice. This choice will be uncomfortable, difficult, and will require you to face your fear. Jack Canfield said, "Everything you want is on the other side of fear..." It is where the magic happens, it is where we grow, it is where we learn, and it is where we can help others face their own fears.

Many believe that asking for help is a sign of weakness. Contrary to belief, it is a sign of strength. It is a sign of courage. Giving up by giving in is a sign of weakness. Never give up, never give in, never surrender has as much to do with the fight in the heat of battle as it does with the quality of your life. When you seek and receive help, things change; and that, my friend, is what this book is about.

From late 1979 to 1993, I had many excuses for why I drank the way I did. I was an expert when it came to the many excuses for being angry all the time. I gave every excuse in the book for why I was an unfriendly asshole that no one wanted to be around. There were many reasons why I was passionate about working in a dangerous job where, at any given moment, my life may be taken from me. Drinking kept me comfortable. My comfort zone was being an alcoholic asshole that nobody enjoyed being around with. I worked at an adrenaline-filled dead-end job to help fill the void in my life. It kept me grounded and prevented me from reliving the terrible memories of the past. The person I had become over the years continued to push the people who loved me away. This allowed me to have the freedom to refrain from answering their silly questions or hear their suggestions that I needed help. By doing this, I was convinced that if the terrorists were to strike again, I wouldn't experience the same pain of losing another comrade. This justification convinced me that the problem was everyone else's and not my own. They just didn't understand the heartache, fear, and agony I felt for so many years. As the feelings resonated within, it prevented me from moving forward. I continued to live in the past as the bad memories replayed day in and day out. I was unable to change until it was important enough for me to find a way.

Family

What can you do to promote world peace?
Go home and love your family.
—Mother Teresa

When you hear the word *family*, what comes to mind? Does the word make you feel amazing, happy, sad, anxious, calm, comforted, etc.? The word *family* can have a variety of meanings, depending on your culture, your upbringing, and your personal experiences. Your family consists of the people who claim you. Whether good or bad, they are the ones who show up regardless.

I consider family to be my surname the family, my wife, and I created, my siblings, parents, grandparents, in-laws, aunts, uncles, cousins, and my close lifelong friends. In their own way, each person contributes to my life. Sociology defines *family* as having the primary responsibility of reproducing society both biologically and socially.

My family is important to me. At every family gathering, there is opportunity for the children and younger family members to learn and grow from the family elders' experiences. As the young learn from the older generation, so do the elders learn from the young. The exchange of stories and experiences is rewarding for both young and old.

If families are who you love, then it should be clear why families are the most important aspect of your life. Each family is different, and this difference is what makes the entire family group so unique. When families break down, many suffer the consequences from the individual to the family to our communities, and in the end, society. One broken link can and will weaken the chain.

My family is very diverse and consists of family members who are white, Hispanic, black, gay, lesbian, and everything in between. What is important to know about my family is regardless of our differences, there is much more that is the same than different. Regardless of our race, religious beliefs, sexual preference, and everything in between, we all want to be loved. We all want to be included, we all want to be heard, and we all want to know there are people who care about our feelings and well-being.

Being a family is difficult. It takes love, hard work, dedication to each other, understanding, devotion, cooperation, and respect. Without these intangibles, families will cease to exist. The family is the haven where each member receives the love and respect that is necessary when it feels as though the entire world has rejected them. Family is the link that connects us to each other as we venture the long journey through life. That bond creates a safe harbor we need to feel that we belong. For me, my family is the key to my heart. My family is not shown in the bloodlines of a family tree but rather by the size of their heart. My family is the reason I needed to change.

Living with Guilt

Every man is guilty of all the good he did not do.

—Voltaire

Guilt is the feeling of remorse or self-reproach one experiences when they feel responsible for a wrong or an offense. We all experience feelings of guilt from time to time and for many different reasons. No one is exempt from this as we all have felt guilt at some point and to some degree. Guilt can and will destroy lives such as when one is found guilty of a crime. Another example of the destructive power guilt has can be found in Shakespeare's *Macbeth* where Lady Macbeth is driven to insanity and ultimately death due to guilt.

Guilt affects people in different ways. Some will become physically ill to the point they are unable to eat and sleep because of their guilt. Some will even take their own life to escape their guilt. Some suffer with their guilt while others learn how to deal with it. Many people will confuse guilt with shame; however, it is easy to distinguish between the two. Guilt is what we feel physically and emotionally for what we do. Shame is what we feel emotionally for what we are or the person we have become. Simply put, it is the difference between what I did versus who I am or have become. Even though shame is a much stronger emotion, both shame and guilt have an immense impact on our perception of self and how we interact with others. One can experience guilt but have no shame or can be full of shame but have no guilt.

I have lived with guilt for a large portion of my adult life. Every day since that early December morning in 1979, I have lived with the feeling of guilt. I believed that I was responsible for my friends' deaths. Prior to the attack, I was working the day shift and my friend John Ball worked evenings. John's and my work schedule had been swapped. I went from days to evenings, which meant John was up front driving the bus that morning, not someone else. This also meant that I was not sitting on the seat I usually sat on; instead, Emil was sitting there.

The emotions I experienced following the attack was a bit of a roller coaster. First, I was happy to be alive but saddened by the death of my close friends. At the same time, I was grateful to be alive but hurt for the families involved. Over time, I began to think more and more about the events that unfolded. I eventually developed a profound sense of remorse for the loss of my comrades that fateful morning. I began to second-guess myself and play the "What if..." and "If I had only..." games, which brought on even deeper feelings of guilt. "If I had only been there" or "I should have seen it coming." These feelings are normal after a traumatic event, and since I did not manage my guilt properly, it completely consumed my life.

Guilt will grind you down to your inner core, eating away every moment of every day as it crushes your spirit and desire to continue in life. If guilt is left unchecked, it can and will destroy you.

In many regards, my guilt was self-punishment, self-imposed for something I believed was my fault. Through many years and unknown amounts of hard work, I have been able to reconcile with my guilt for the events that occurred on that December morning. Do not wait to say the things that need to be said. Do not wait to do the things that need to be done. Losing someone before saying what needs to be said or doing what needs to be done will result in feelings of guilt that will destroy you from the inside out. Living with guilt can and will ultimately lead to your own demise.

Getting Started

Your Story, Your Journey

Everyone has a story to tell. Do you know yours? Have you even thought about yours? Have you ever noticed that the best and most interesting speakers are those that don't just tell their stories, they live them? I have come to realize that many people do not see their own life as a story worth telling. In fact, many of them don't even see life as a story they have lived. Many people wake up, drudge through their day, and for the most part, passively accept how their day unfolds. Just as they drift through life aimlessly, they find themselves drifting in and out of their own story as if they were seaweed floating whichever way the ocean currents push them.

Then there are individuals that have it so "together." They are extremely organized almost as if they were obsessive-compulsive about every minute of every day. These individuals have every single minute in their life accounted for. These individuals make sure that even the extra five minutes of sleep is noted in their daily planner. Every single minute of every single day matters to this person, even if those minutes are determined and spent on someone else's agenda. Not only is every minute accounted for, but they are accounted for by someone else's priorities and agenda.

Today is the day you wake up to your own story. Today is the day you realize the power you have inside to live a better life by being intentional with every action you choose to do. When you look at life as a story, you will make choices to write the story you want instead of just accepting the life handed to you by others. When you decide to write your own life story, you are no longer a character in someone else's novel. You become the hero of your own life, in your own epic novel.

Speaker and entrepreneur Jim Rohn said, "One of the best places to start to turn your life around is by doing whatever appears on your mental 'I should' list." The most important aspect to change is the actions we choose. Without you taking action, nothing happens. Without action, we stay dormant in our life journey. When you act, the first change you will see is in yourself.

In your life, it will never be the tangible items you acquire that make you valuable. What you become in the process of change is what will bring value to your life. When you begin to take the essential and necessary actions, you will begin to convert your dreams into reality. There is no other source that will provide you with the personal value that you will gain when you decide to act. When you act on what you value, those values become clear permanent priorities.

The action you take gives you the moral authority and confidence needed to live your life the way you believe you should. The actions you make become the foundation of your character. No longer will you be a passive person allowing your character to be influenced by others. The actions and decisions we make manifest the character that lives within all of us. It is up to you to build the positive lifestyle that you can and will maintain. What is important to understand is that contentment is only found when you are where you are supposed to be in life. Contentment comes when your actions are in sync with who you are.

Being the hero in your own life story doesn't always mean you get your way. True heroes always sacrifice for the greater good. When you are writing yourself in as the hero of your life story, remember, heroes choose to make sacrifices. Heroes have reasons for their actions; they are not the characters in someone else's story. They become the story.

- *When you think about your life story, how do you see yourself?*
- *How do you see yourself conquering the problems we all must face?*

- *How do you see yourself handling life's many challenges?*
- *How do you measure your own potential?*
- *What have you learned from your life experiences?*
- *How well have you written your own life story?*

We all have a story that has been formatted by the actions we have made. Actions yield results. Often, we manipulate our stories to ourselves, our family, and our friends so we may appear to live larger than we really are. Everyone knows the old fishing story where the fish grows larger each time we tell the story. Now, with so many social media outlets, many of us share with the world our personally construed self-image and adventure. We piece our reality together then weave them into intricate tales of action-packed adventures that reinvents our past while imagining our future and missing the present story in the middle. Regardless of how we perceive and change our stories, these tales are an important aspect of our lives. Our stories demonstrate our ability to make sense out of life, which is why there are millions of stories that need to be told. With each passing moment, a new narrative is written. Every person has a story that contains suffering, loss, pain, adventure, success, and greatness. Our libretto as a people, the song of which we all sing, is a culmination of each of us as we tell the stories, trusting our stories, listening carefully to the stories of others, revising, writing, editing, starting over, creating new stories, and then delicately weaving it all together. Our life stories bring us together.

Your life story is a self-portrait of who you are placed into words. You are much more than the author or leading character, you are the storyteller who can spin how your story is told. The way you spin your story reveals much about the way you see yourself. Often, this is true even when your story veers from the actual life you have lived. Are you the victim or the victor? The hero or the villain?

The moment you were born and breathed your first breath, your story began. As we progressed through childhood, we began listening to stories from our parents. As we listened to their stories, we began to engrave their storytelling talent deep inside, mimicking verbal and nonverbal language. As children, we began to develop our own stories that included tales of imaginary adventures of slaying the dragon for the greater good, of being swept away by a knight in shining armor, or of being lost in space as we traveled to distant stars. As we grow older, these stories begin to have more truth to them as we begin to listen more intricately to our elders and pass them on to others. As we grow still older, we begin to manipulate our own stories about ourselves, our families, and experiences. As young adults, our stories become more realistic as continued truth about family, friends, and experiences begin to fill our tales. These are the stories that help explain who we are, where we have come from, and where we fit in. Even though our stories appear to be similar, every tale we tell is not the same. Every life has a unique story, and it is up to the individual to share it.

Think about how unique your life story really is. There are well over seven billion people on this planet we call home, and there is no one else like you. Your story includes your upbringing, your life challenges, the lessons you have learned, every experience, every achievement, failures, and all the gifts you have ever received. Your story includes everything in your life right up to this very moment as you read this book. With all this in mind, think about the millions of moments and the series of events that has led up to everyone you have encountered on your journey. Have you ever wondered who they are deep inside? Or where they come from? Or what they long for in life? Or what makes them tick? The simple question is, have you ever asked? The better question is, will you ever take the time to ask?

What makes life so interesting is that it is made up of a tapestry of people who weave in and out of our lives. I think the saying goes "People come into your life for a reason, a season, or a lifetime." Everyone has something to offer or share, but so many of us don't make time to find out what that is. How much more interesting would life be if every person you encountered, regardless of how fleeting the moment, is treated as an opportunity for an intriguing story ready to be told? The next time a person is standing before you, no matter who they are—young or old, rich or poor, angry or kind— imagine them as a best-selling author just waiting to have their story heard. Do you care enough about others to listen? Are you interested enough in what can be learned from others to ask that person in front of you "Who are you? What's your story?" I know that is difficult to imagine and possibly awkward to do, but… What if you started a conversation by saying, "So, I'd love to ask you something, and I'm not asking a rhetorical question. I really want to know…"

- *Where were you born?*
- *Where do you live now?*
- *What makes you smile?*
- *What is the most important life lesson you've learned so far?*
- *What is your deepest fear?*
- *What is your greatest dream for your life?*
- *Who are you?*

The problem with this seems to be it is something not everyone is comfortable enough to try. Starting a conversation with someone may be the difference between life and death for them. What if the person you stopped to talk with felt no one cared about them and was considering suicide? But because you took just a moment in time to ask that person about their life, showing them that you genuinely care, may have saved their life. The same could be true with you. Maybe taking the time to ask that one simple question ends up saving your life.

When I talk with people about their life story, I always get similar responses, "I don't have time to think about it," "I don't have a story anyone would be interested in," "I don't know where to start," "I have a hard-enough time just getting by, I can't be thinking about life stories." President Theodore Roosevelt once famously said, "Do what you can, with what you have, where you are." In other words, just start. You have everything you need to get started, and since you are the author of your personal journey, you can write in the parts you want and delete the things that don't serve your story.

Start right where you are—right here, right now. Open your eyes to see that your opportunity is always present, wherever you are.

Think about it: look at your life and where you are right now. What are some opportunities that you see? Start with the one thing you do better than anyone else. If you don't know what that is, search for it and find it. Find that one thing and start mastering it. Start with the words you use and how they affect not only yourself but others around you. What we say to ourselves either encourages us through our journey, pushing us to achieve more or discourages us, stopping us dead in our tracks. Make a commitment to yourself today to only use positive words of encouragement. Watch how these positive words change the way you act and feel. What will you tell yourself each day to get your day started?

The easiest way to start is to make minor changes within. These changes over time will grow and yield big results. The minor changes in how you think, in what you read, in your speech, or in your habits will begin to snow ball, creating a much larger outcome. What are some of the minor changes that you can make in your life today that will help you improve your ability to make a difference tomorrow?

Stories may not seem that important; however, research has shown that our brains naturally tell stories to give structure and meaning to our lives. This same research also found that stories shape our lives and personalities, which is a key link in how we define who we are. We all have our one favorite tale of our own life journey. This story not only helps us to make sense of our previous experiences but also gives us a sense of self. Over our lifetime, we are constantly adding, updating, amending, and editing our life's journey as we encounter new experiences and interact with new people.

Your life journey is a continuous piece of work in progress, constantly evolving and changing over time. It is up to you to make it positive. You are the conductor, and your life is a masterful symphony with a beautiful sound. As we grow and mature into adulthood, the decisions we make grow increasingly complex as the addition of new characters play an intricate part of how we develop. As we venture through life, many of our stories continue to unfold as we take a turn to a softer, gentler, and for the most part a happier tale. I believe this happens over our lifetime as we go from surviving as young renegades to thriving as successful individuals. In the end, our stories reflect the improvements we have experienced gradually over our lifetime becoming more heartfelt as they relay lessons of understanding and wisdom.

Initially, I asked, what is your story? Simply put, your life story is the culmination of all your experiences wrapped into a small box with a beautiful bow ready to be presented to St. Peter at the grand gates of heaven. Is this box something you are proud of? Consider this: your life story is an epic novel that is overflowing with dozens of chapters of your experiences. Within each of those chapters, your actions, experiences, and the wealth of wisdom you have gained fill each page. Will you share it? Each person who hears your story or reads your novel will gain a different lesson from different chapters. However, this wealth of wisdom will never be passed on if you don't share your life's testimony. Just as you have been inspired by others who share their amazing yet inspirational journey, you too can inspire others by telling your own.

So where do you begin? The optimal place to start is to begin brainstorming about an experience you have told that may benefit others. Maybe start with a story from your youth or high school days. Remember, the greatest and most influential stories come from the heart. Barry Lopez, an award-winning American novelist, said it best when he stated, "If stories come to you, care for them. And learn to give them away where they are needed. Sometimes, a person needs a story more than food to stay alive." When you think about it, there is more to life than just working to earn the almighty paycheck. There is more to you than how you are defined by your actions, career, or social media accounts. You have great wisdom and knowledge within that needs to be shared. Start sharing your story today.

Define Your OWN Relationships

By changing yourself, you can change your relationships. This may be a difficult task as it may mean that ending certain relationships are necessary. Have you ever found yourself wishing your parents, your child, or maybe your partner were different? Another way to ask this question is, have you ever found yourself thinking if they were just more X, or Y, or Z, life would be much easier and more fulfilling? You would be much happier if you are honest with yourself when you think about this: we HAVE ALL DONE IT.

You might be happier for a brief time, but chances are, you will return to where you started as you find other faults in your relationships. Will the other individual be any happier trying to fit into your set of expectations, both spoken and unspoken? Take a moment and think about this. Why do you think if someone changes to meet your expectations and standards, you will be any happier than you are now? Other individuals and materialistic objects do not give you enjoyment and neither making you feel fulfilled. Only YOU can make YOURSELF feel the happiness and enjoyment that life has to offer.

Have you ever felt disappointed by another person when they did not react the way you had hoped they would? Surely, if they cared enough about you, they would know you needed…whatever it is you need. They should just know, right? But they do not, which results in anger and resentment building up deep inside your consciousness. The only one you should be angered with and resent is yourself. It is unreasonable to expect that anyone should be able to read your mind, even though that is what most of us seem to believe. We assume the other person knows what we desire, what we need, or what we are thinking. There are many ways to express your needs and desires instead of expecting others to be a mind reader and know how to please you emotionally, financially, and physically.

Consider this example. Your neighbor just dumped off their kids at your house for an afternoon playdate because you work at home. You have a tight deadline, and thanks to your neighbor, you will have to work late to complete your tasks that need to be completed on time. That feeling of being taken advantage of builds resentment and frustration. How do you believe this situation should have been handled differently? What should have been done or said differently so you did not feel like your neighbor had taken you for granted?

First, learn the power of saying NO. Learning how to say no can transform your life by giving you the autonomy to prioritize your own tasks and time to complete them rather than adapting to the agendas of other people. Saying no does not imply that you are an asshole or a jerk; rather, it implies that you are sticking to your own priorities by creating boundaries that you have set for yourself. You need to complete your work that has a firm deadline. This also means the after-work happy hour may need to be cancelled so you may complete your important tasks. Relationships present difficult issues that we all, at some point or another, will experience with those around us. What I have found is that when we try to change the people around us, often, we end up exhausted, frustrated, and disappointed.

What if I told you there is a better way to improve your relationships that will make both parties happier and much less stressed? When I tell you the answer to the previous question, most people will not believe it. The answer is simple, IT STARTS WITH YOU! The immediate reaction to my answer from others is typically, "It's not me, it's everyone else! They just don't understand me," as they shout from the rooftops for all to hear as the unwillingness to change becomes obvious. There are many ways you can start to empower yourself to improve your relationships. It all starts with you taking the actions that are necessary to make it happen, which, for some, is the hardest thing they will ever do. Many of us hate the thought of being alone in the world, and this fear keeps us drowning in relationships that ultimately keep us from thriving. For me, I enjoy my alone time, but I don't want to live a life where I'm completely alone. Over the years, I have come to realize that there are certain behaviors and character traits we all have that might be pushing away the very people we want to keep close. These behaviors and traits require immediate attention that is necessary for us to grow and develop positive relationships.

I know from personal experience that over the years, I have pushed away many people I care deeply about. Looking back to the time between 1979 and 1993, I can identify the exact moments when I pushed people away while I was dealing with my demons. During that time, I was on the verge of losing everything including the people I cared for most. Even today, I continue to find myself pushing people away. I have been told that this habit of pushing people away is not all my fault, and often, the old saying "It takes two to tango" holds a true meaning. Yes, it does take two people to trigger an argument; on the other hand, it also takes two people to create a solution that solves a disagreement. But if you have the same mind-set as I did for over fourteen years, you probably are thinking, "Why should I change? Why should I make the first move? I'm not the one with a problem. Why me?" This type of reactive thinking can damage a relationship beyond repair.

If you believe you can change the people around you to be the way you want, YOU WILL FAIL! Trying to manipulate them to fit the mold of exactly the person you are insisting they become will only end in wasted energy and frustration BECAUSE YOU WILL FAIL.

An advantageous means to spending your time and energy wisely is to place your effort on improving yourself, becoming the best person you can be. Most of us are blind at improving ourselves and continue to dwell on the idea that it is an unfair notion to have to change ourselves. But if you took the time to detach yourself from a given situation and place it under a microscope, you will find the aspects that need improvement. It doesn't take much to see the changes that need action and, once they are addressed appropriately, will yield the results you are seeking. This, in turn, will reap major rewards in the relationships you wish to improve.

By improving yourself, you increase your personal value. When you improve your own personal value, you will increase the value you place on others. No one likes feeling criticized or undervalued. When I work with people through a process of self-empowerment and discovery, many find that the people in their inner circle are holding them back, creating a sense of feeling not valuable. The obstacles in their path, whether intrinsic or extrinsic, prevents them from achieving excellence. It might be time to find a new support system that puts forth what you need to succeed rather than taming the lion within. The most difficult facet of this process is deciding on how to begin. I suggest you begin by minimizing the tasks, prioritize what is important, and attack foreseen successes. Minimize. Prioritize. Attack! By minimizing the tasks first, you will begin to develop an itemized list of importance. Once this list is created, you attack! Once you achieve these small victories, you begin to create a positive mind-set. You will then begin to feel encouraged to continue rather than discontinuing as the larger tasks are often too difficult to achieve.

Right now, you might be feeling as if your family and friends walk all over you as though you are a doormat. STOP BEING A DOORMAT! It is time to become assertive and learn how to set boundaries that will bring the changes you are looking for in your life. The best part of this approach is you don't have to share this with others; you just need to learn how to be assertive and set boundaries.

It is time to work on building your confidence. Again, minimize the tasks and begin on how to say no. Next, begin to prioritize your desires and your expectations in order. Once this is complete, you will find your happiness will increase. The concerns you have about others and how they should be will decrease. When your happiness and sense of self-worth increases, your relationships with others will change. Remember, YOU and ONLY YOU have the power to change YOU.

When you have time to spare, go to your local bookstore. Browse the endless aisles of books until you stumble upon the self-improvement section. You will quickly realize the number of self-help guides on relationships are not in short supply. Why do you think that is? I have asked myself and others this same question many times. I believe people are looking to not only better themselves but also the people that make up their relationships. However, you don't need to spend years studying, highlighting, and footnoting all those manuals if you simply focus on yourself. Pause and take a moment to focus on where you are in your life at this present moment. DO IT! Focus on where your life is at this very moment.

Self-Empowerment and Discovery Journey Exercise

Write down what you realized about you when you focused on where your life is at this moment. Now, write a list of all the THINGS you want to change in your life. You notice I said THINGS, not people. Many write down things like "I wish I had a better relationship with my kids" or "I wish I was more valued at work" or "I wish my partner and I were closer." Doing this will help you identify areas that need to be addressed immediately. Once the problems are identified, create the correct strategies needed to place you on the path that will get you to where you want to be. In other words, once you write these things down, you have bullet points to develop strategies that will help you achieve your goals. If one of the items, you wrote down was "I want a better relationship with my coworkers." You need to first look at where the friction points are with your coworkers and then come up with solutions to help you improve yourself with regards to those friction points. Once this occurs, create a prioritized plan of action that will transform these changes into habits and, ultimately, a positive work environment. Remember you can only change you.

Dale Carnegie's book *How to Win Friends and Influence People*, which if you haven't read you should, has inspired and educated millions of people on the secrets about how to improve their relationships in every area of their lives, from successfully dealing with colleagues to having a happy family. In the book, Carnegie presents a list of three principles of fundamental techniques in handling people, which is just as relevant today as it was the day it was published in 1936.

This list contains the following bullet points:

- "Don't criticize, condemn or complain."
- "Give honest and sincere appreciation."
- "Arouse in the other person eager want."

People who have read the book believe they will learn top secret business advice that only successful people know. But Dale Carnegie's main points listed above work in every relationship you will develop. Point three, I believe, is the most crucial: you can only convince people to do what you want them to do by giving them what they desire most.

Consider this this example: You want that raise or a promotion that will help you live more comfortably. When desiring this increase in salary, most people storm into their boss's office and demand a raise. While taking this approach may work for some, many people fall short. Instead of voicing your demands to your superiors, try a different approach. Leave your pride, ego, and aspirations at the door and present a list of exactly how you have benefitted the company and how you plan to improve on these accomplishments. Use objective numbers such as profit gained, reduction in overhead cost, and how many relationships you have built with other companies to show how your efforts have been an asset to the company. By doing this, you will create a win-win scenario for both you and your boss. If you show your boss examples of how the company will continue to benefit from your work, it becomes much easier to obtain the result you are hoping for. Make the change about the betterment of the company and how it will continue to benefit the team, not you.

Here is another way to think about it: If your partner smokes cigarettes, complaining about the smell, mess, and cost will probably do nothing to change their habit. In fact, it will likely just cause a lot of arguments. However, if you leave brochures around about the great vacations you can take if you had some extra money compared with the total cost of smoking every month, they might see that their money is literally going up in smoke. Consider this: if you are spending $40 a week on your smokes over a year or fifty-two weeks, that's $2,080 you are spending. You can do the same thing with a partner who drinks. You both know you need a new car that you think you cannot afford. DO THE MATH FOR THEM. If they are going out every weekend and drinking, they may be spending $200 a week on liquid entertainment. At the end of the year, this will add up to $10,400 a year. When it is objectively placed into terms that people understand, they quickly see the benefit of cutting back.

Respectable manners cost you nothing; unpleasant ones can and will cost you everything. It is imperative to be polite to everyone, even in your own home with family members. NO ONE LIKES BEING DISSED, especially in their own home.

When I was a teenager, my father told me many times, "You are judged by the company you keep." I did not fully understand his statement until I joined the Navy. This is when I realized that the person you become is correlated with the type of people you socialize with. Whether you believe it or not, dating, marriage, military life, living in another country, or hanging with the wrong crowd will change you, and it is not always for the better. You might find yourself going with the flow of someone else's negative behavior just for the sake of the relationship, to impress them or to show them you are qualified to be a "FIT" in that person's life. I saw this in the military where people, myself included, would drink just to fit in, to be accepted. Looking back, I realize that I did not need to drink to fit in. The next time you *"just want to fit in"* ask yourself these questions:

- *Is it worth sacrificing who you are so you can fit in?*
- *Is it worth sacrificing who you are for the sake of keeping someone in your life who is a cancer to your own persona, who does not encourage you to be more, and who keeps you from being your best self?*
- *Is it worth the effort to keep someone in your life who is no more than an obstacle that keeps you stranded in your life?*

For some, the questions above are very difficult to answer. I know many of you may not be honest when answering them. It is hard to say no or cut off a cancerous relationship that leads you down a path to failure. This reminds me of a TV commercial where a young woman wearing a skintight pair of white pants asks her male partner, "Does my butt look big in these jeans?" I do not know about you, but that seems like it could be a dangerous question to answer. For men, this is a trick question that brings terror and requires a great deal of diplomacy. If he says no, she will not feel beautiful as she may begin to believe she has a flat ass or that he is a liar and is saying what she wants to hear. On the contrary, if he says yes, she will become furious as thoughts of obesity fill her self-image. After over forty-one years of marriage and learning on the job, the correct answer is, "You look great, but those jeans are not cut right for you. Maybe try another brand?" The wrong but brutally honest answer would be "No, the pants don't make you look fat. Your fat makes you look fat. It's time for you to start taking better care of your health."

I hope by now you have noticed that it is important to be your true self, not who others want you to be. This is no easy task considering our culture enables us to be someone who we are not by creating false popular self-images through social media. We become this image that other people desire as we continuously post to social media with hopes of pleasing others with who we are. The sad part about this is you gain self-worth, believing you are being accepted by making people happy through your posts as you live minute to minute, waiting for each person to hit the "like" button. At the end of the day, does this make you happy that you feel accepted by how many "likes" you have on a Facebook post? Furthermore, are you pleasing yourself or are you living to please others? Pleasing others at the sake of your own fulfillment leads to a term I like to use, "people pleasing." IF YOU ARE A PEOPLE PLEASER, STOP BEING ONE. People pleasers have few boundaries and do not know how to say no. They get dumped on, they get imposed upon and are totally exhausted. They develop a self-image on social media outlets that many people believe is amazing. Most times, they are running on an empty gas tank with few of their needs being met and are unfulfilled. IF THIS IS YOU, it is time to reconsider this cycle and move forward on your own journey, working toward your own dreams.

If you are trapped in a relationship pothole, I hope I have presented you some ideas about how you can improve and continue to positively grow your relationships. From this day forward, stop looking externally at others and take a closer look at yourself. Taking a hard look at yourself will make a big difference in your life. There is no doubt that relationships with parents, children, lovers, friends, and colleagues can bring out the worst in us, or the best in us. It is your choice. Who do you want to be from this point forward? I am betting that you want to be your best self, with more confidence, honesty, and integrity. The type of person others will want to develop positive long-lasting relationships with.

Purpose Driven

Have you ever experienced a moment in your life when you felt everything was perfect? A moment when everything was connected as if your life purpose was exactly whatever it was that you were doing at that moment? People who have experienced this describe this feeling as a sense of being alive, being intentional, or being able to clearly know that their actions are exactly in line with what they were meant to do. Many describe this feeling as being totally absorbed where time seems to disappear as you live in the moment. What I have found over the years is that there are many people who do not experiences this feeling. If they do experience it, they only have this sense for a few fleeting moments in their life. For some, this feeling is unrecognizable, and they're unable to distinguish what it represents. This feeling of drive is letting you know you are working in your purpose, what you are supposed to do with your life. People who can connect with their purpose find true meaning in life. They are the ones turning lemons into lemonade. When you are engaged in your purpose, you are better able to handle life's ups and downs.

When you connect with your purpose, your mind is better able to guard against life challenges that tend to derail you. Even in the most difficult of times, a person with a powerful sense of purpose remains satisfied with life. When you connect with your purpose, your priorities become clear. Having a purpose helps you create a vision that enables you to determine whether you will be successful in life or not. We are all on a life journey, and knowing our purpose enables us to select the path that leads to the destination we want. When we have a purpose, we know the correct path that is required to arrive at our destination. Without purpose, we bounce around in life developing a "jack-of-all-trades" persona, letting others determine where we will end up.

I firmly believe we are all born with a purpose defined deep inside of us. That purpose is what we were born to do, and it begins with a dream, a life dream so strong it cannot be denied. If you pay attention to your life dream, you will begin heading down the path of your success journey. The way you know your dream is authentic is by knowing what you are willing to sacrifice to achieve it. Once you discover your purpose, your life changes forever.

As a kid, I never gave purpose a second thought. Purpose was something given to me, provided by either my parents, teachers, or others close to me. I went to school, I made good grades, I hung out with my friends, I went to practice, I had fun, and then I went to sleep. Each day was placed on rewind every night and repeated daily until I graduated. After graduating from high school, my earlier purpose disappeared. I was left on my own to find my purpose that would fill the void left deep inside after graduating. It is at this point, as we transition from adolescent to adulthood, where many of us run into trouble as we stumble our way into our next chapter. We are unable to fill this void of purposeful security that was provided to us by society and our parents. We began with a handout, being told what to do daily, then cut off to learn how to fend for ourselves in the real world. Many people fail to find purpose and continue living a life where handouts are provided to them as they drift aimlessly through life without resolution.

When you become determined about finding your own purpose, life changes. Once you find your purpose, you make it yours, owning it every step of the way. Your inner drive becomes activated, which cares less about the thoughts and opinions of others. Approval from others is not a requirement for you to live in your own purpose. I can guarantee you this: once you become determined about the path of your life, you will find your purpose. When you live your life intentionally determined, you will experience an incredible feeling of fulfillment that words cannot describe. This feeling of fulfillment will become overwhelming, and you will know in that moment that you have found your purpose.

The Man in the Mirror

Self-reflection is a vital component of living a successful life. Socrates stated, "The unexamined life is not worth living." Unfortunately, we are often consumed with the continuing cascades of noise and distortion, the day-to-day distractions and constant information overload. With all the distractions, it becomes difficult to find opportunities for self-reflection. Through self-reflection, you can determine if you are working toward your goals. You will be able to determine if your aspirations are being met or if what you are working for allows opportunities to personally grow your dreams and visions without becoming conflicted with your daily routines. Most importantly, it will answer the following questions: "How do you treat yourself? Do you truly listen to your inner voice? Do you encourage yourself often?" Without self-reflection, you will never know if you are spending more time and attention on your surroundings rather than on yourself and your ambitions.

Deciding to make changes corresponds with the desire to do more with your life, become more in your life, and to seek a different outcome in your life. Once you address that feeling of change that tells you it is time to stop replacing your dreams with fear, you will advance. If life went along exactly how you scripted it, you would miss the opportunity to find the boundaries of your capabilities and limits of your internal strengths. Without self-reflection, you will never achieve your full capacity to learn new things or what limits are placed on your own self-endurance. Reflecting on the challenges we face lets us know what we are doing correct in our life, what we are doing wrong that requires attention, and what actions are necessary to fix the items that need to be changed. If you don't take time to reflect on your challenges, you will never know what your strengths and weaknesses are. To be successful, you must be willing to consider your past and look beyond where you're at right now. By reflecting on your past, you can evaluate what worked to create the desired changes and what did not. Knowing what works and what does not helps you to fully understand your strengths and weaknesses as it enables you to move past your shortcomings and move forward to a period of innovative ideas.

A powerful moment of self-reflection, for me, happened in 1993 when I sat alone on the edge of my bed, knowing there was a choice I needed to make. I reflected on the changes in my life that needed to be addressed or, with the simple pull of the trigger, end the pain and hopelessness I experienced for so many years. Only through self-reflection was I able to make the choice to continue with my life. The only way that I was able to make the right choice was through the honesty of my self-reflection of the events and experiences that merged together in this defining moment of my life. Self-reflection enabled me to see the changes that were necessary to move forward and find purpose. Through self-reflection, I realized I needed help and found the courage to ask and accept it. I needed to be committed at making the correct changes needed in my life that would bring me out of the darkness of considering suicide. Self-reflection showed my strengths and the weaknesses that required further growth so I could move forward and be the man, father, and husband I needed to be.

I realized, through the process of self-reflecting—as you too may realize—I wasn't living the life I desired. You too may realize the demons talking in your head can be silenced and come to an understanding that there is no need to continually relive unwelcoming memories of past experiences. You too may realize that you need help dealing with your feelings of being overwhelmed and outnumbered. Without self-reflection, you will never realize that there are necessary changes in your life needed to take advantage of your strengths while improving on your weaknesses. If you are not committed to self-reflection of your past, you will never be able to move forward and grow as an individual into a future of success. Only through self-reflection did I come to realize that giving up by giving in is a sign of weakness. Only by looking in the mirror and reflecting on the person I had become did I realize that asking for help was necessary and was not a sign of weakness but rather a show of strength.

When I interviewed Dr. Dorothy Bonvillain on my *Success an Intentional Lifestyle Radio Show*, we discussed the value of helping lift others up. Dr. Bonvillain explained during the interview how, through her work, she helps military families move from surviving to thriving. She analyzed how she found her purpose and passion through self-reflection of her forty-five-years of experience as a military spouse. Achieving success can be distilled down to how much you help others. When you find a way to serve others, it will lead to great wealth, great power, and profound influence. I believe President John F. Kennedy said it best when he stated, "Don't ask what your country can do for you, but what you can do for your country."

Another guest on my show, Tim Davis, had a profound impact on many people who heard the interview. He told his story of growing up in the projects as an at-risk kid, what it is like to live in poverty, and how chasing your dream can fixate you on a path to achievement. The lessons Tim expressed through his personal stories demonstrated it's acceptable to fail. His life story demonstrates that anyone can become successful by overcoming significant adversities. He is proof that through self-reflection, you can gain clarity about what is important, that you can improve your performance when you find your strengths and weaknesses, and that you can grow meaningful relationships with others when you develop a better understanding of yourself. Tim also proved to me during our interview that success is measured in numerous ways. For some, success means having a significant amount of money; for others, it means having the big house with a white picket fence. But for Tim, it meant never going hungry again.

What does success look like to you? When you ask yourself what it means to "live well," what is your answer? Considering there are so many beliefs that have become a part of who you are, living well can be a difficult concept to fully embrace. To understand what success looks like to you, it is important to examine your beliefs. Do you believe that living well means possessing luxury items like a new car and a large home, or do you believe that living well means being able to spend more time at home and less time at work? How do your beliefs support your vision for yourself, and how do they hinder it? Only through self-reflection will you be able to answer these questions. To begin this process, start by closing your eyes and imagining an ideal day where you spend your time pursuing your passions and living a simpler life. As you examine your beliefs, ask yourself why you believe something to be true. You may discover, through this process, you've held on to a belief for the simple reason of never questioning it.

Another interview with guest Jack Perry Jr. also had an outstanding impact on those who heard the interview. He taught us that fear and anger are connected. Furthermore, it is important to understand what causes these feelings of anger and fear while creating an understanding of why they are connected. While speaking with Jack, I learned that my anger was motivated by my desire not to experience guilt, hurt, or fear. I recognized that I used anger for many years to build a wall around my survivor's guilt. He taught me that it was an emotion I used to hide my pain, guilt, and self-blame that had become locked inside for so many years. What I understand now about my own anger is that it kept me shackled and confined to a lonely place deep within that did not allow me to grow into the man I needed to be. Not until I faced my anger and guilt was I able to move forward.

Anger is a natural response the human body uses during the fight aspect of our subconscious fight-or-flight response. This is our body's sympathetic response to danger. Do we run from a dangerous situation, or do we fight back? You may not always have the option to fight what threatens you, but you have anger, which is one of the ways that we help our body prepare for potential danger. If anger goes unchecked, the result can and will lead to violence. When you spend time reflecting on your anger, you will realize that you must change by analyzing the situation. If you are an angry person, and anger is born out of fear, reflect on what is causing fear in your life.

When you self-reflect, you look inward. This is an opportunity for you to stand in front of the mirror and ask yourself, "Who am I?" Self-reflection is about you, no one else, and only you can self-reflect about yourself. When you look inward, you build self-awareness and self-regulation. This allows you to understand your deepest emotions, greatest strengths, weaknesses, motivators, values, and goals. By doing this, you will understand how they impact your ability to achieve success. Self-regulation is your ability to control or redirect your disruptive emotions, impulsive behaviors, and the negative voices that try to control your every thought. Self-regulation enables you to adapt to change when facing the tough challenges life throws at you. Building self-awareness and self-regulation will directly impact your ability in achieving lasting success in your life. With strong self-awareness and self-regulation, you build confidence, which is crucial for achieving the success you desire.

> *The more you reflect on your strengths and weaknesses, the more confident you will be, the more determined you will become. The more determined you become, the more intentional you will be. The more intentional you are, the more likely you are to achieve lasting success in your life.*

Take a moment, review the last statement, and write it down for future reference. Put in a place where you will see it every day. As you continue down your life journey, return to the above statement you wrote down as it will become a vital tool at any given moment.

When you don't feel confident, revert to this statement and self-reflect on who you are and where you want to be. When you lack confidence in yourself, skills, and craft, it shows. If you don't have confidence in yourself, who else will? Your level of self-confidence is related to your ability to handle pressure under stressful situations. The lack of self-confidence may undermine your efforts before you even start. It is important to remember that having this form of confidence refers to your sense of self, knowing who you are and what you are capable of. It is essentially how you view yourself in the world around you. You do this through self-reflection. If you have a low sense of self-confidence, you may not believe you have anything to offer and contribute to the world, your loved ones, or anyone else. Lack of self-confidence will prevent you from living the life you envisioned for yourself while letting others control the one you have.

Jennifer Stevenson, another guest on my radio show, discussed the importance of developing a purpose and having confidence to achieve your dreams. Her story showed us that even while living under the darkness of poverty and while obstructed with a learning disability, you can still achieve the success you envision. During the show, Jennifer reminded us, "If you can learn one thing from her, just know that everything in your life will come together to bring you to your purpose." Self-reflection will help you find your purpose, and when you find it, approval from others will no longer hold value. The only approval you need is what you obtain through self-reflection.

A common thread between all the guests I have interviewed on my radio show is this:

> *To be successful requires discipline; it requires hard work, self-awareness, confidence, and not being afraid to ask for help.*

The discipline of self-reflection is the secret to understanding yourself and purpose. Regardless of what career path you choose, develop a drive and passion to be the best you can be. This will only happen with discipline and hard work. Sure, it is easy to give up a night of class or study to watch TV or even go to the local bar with your friends, but if you want to achieve success and earn good grades, you must do the necessary actions to move you in the right direction. In Malcolm Gladwell's book *Outliers*, he looked at several great achievers such as the Beatles, Steve Jobs, Bill Gates; and what he found is that in all cases, over ten thousand hours of practice was completed in achieving the level of mastery associated with each of the world-class achievers he studied. He found this was even true with prodigies such as Mozart. How many hours have you put in on what you are trying to achieve? How many hours have you put in on yourself? How many hours have you spent self-reflecting?

The more consistent you are at spending time in self-reflection, the more you will be able to live your life with absolute clarity. In today's world, it is so easy to be distracted throughout the day only to discover that you have spent little time on your priorities. By self-reflecting, you can stay focused on your priorities and learn to let go of the busy work that steals your time and knocks you off course.

One of the hardest things you will have to do is narrow down your priority list to match the vision you are trying to achieve. Spending time to reflect on your actions and goals will save you from spending your day being busy with nothing to show for it. Self-reflection will enable you to truly prioritize and become more intentional. By doing this, importance will be placed on self-reflection and essential actions you need to perform to succeed.

Many people drift through life without direction, intention, or purpose. How do you know you are on the right course? What are the most important strengths you have? Is there one characteristic that is more important than any other? These questions can be answered through self-reflection and help provide the ability to monitor your emotions and reactions.

Through self-reflection, you will keep yourself grounded; you will become attuned to new opportunities and be more able to pivot your actions toward what you are trying to achieve. When you become grounded, you are deliberate in what you are attempting to achieve and attuned to new opportunities. When you can control your mind and emotions, you develop a sense of ownership of your self-knowledge of success.

There is no doubt self-reflection can be difficult to master, but once you grasp this concept, you will know and understand your capabilities. You will be able to acknowledge your emotional triggers. At any given point, you will be able to immediately identify the emotions that are keeping you from personal development. Once you master self-reflection, you will be able to embrace your intuition and learn how to take risks by trusting your instinct. Once mastered, you will become more disciplined in every area of your life, which will help you to remain focused on your goal. Over time, you will be able to block out distractions and remain focused for extended periods. When you know your strengths and weaknesses, your control over your emotions will improve and begin to develop different perspective of situations you are facing while remaining confident.

Often, when we look to a new life and a new vision, it entails acquiring important tangible and nontangible attributes that will help you succeed. Before you take the necessary steps to add more to your life you need to assess what you already own by reflecting on your personal belongings as well as your personal attributes. Chances are, you will find you already have what you need to take the steps toward a promising future. It is very possible you will discover that you already have everything you need to bring about the changes you want in your life.

Disliked? Who Cares!

Just when the caterpillar thought the world
was over, it became a butterfly.

—English Proverb

From a very young age, most of us are educated in the art of people-pleasing. The idea that there are advantages of being disliked is probably a new concept for many of us. The biggest advantage to this idea is that it allows us to become our authentic self, shaking off the shackles of society's expectations as we forge our own destinies. There are many advantages to being disliked and unpopular, and it is up to you to decide whether you want to accept it. Here are just a few pros:

Being True to Yourself

You may wish to be popular and the life of the party at work or school, but popularity is not as enduring as being true to yourself. Being true to yourself means making the smart choice at the right time that will allow you to look in the mirror each day and be proud of what you see.

Not Bowing to Societal Pressure

The idea of being ourselves can be almost unthinkable when we are children as we bow to our parents' wishes, receiving the amount of praise we desire. We are also prone to allowing peer pressure to consume our inner being, even when we know it is wrong. "But everyone is doing it" is a popular excuse many of us use. Millions of people on this planet use heroin, but does that make it a valid lifestyle choice any sane person would wish to make? The answer is no, yet many people experiment and become addicted to illegal drugs due to the peer pressure from others.

Setting Your Own Goals

By listening to the naysayers who might have wrote you off as useless, you are free to set your own goals and expectations. Being told you can never do something is often the needed inspiration required to achieve exactly what they say you will never be able to accomplish. It is fun to defy the expectations and prove them wrong.

Achieving Your Dreams

Many people discuss and elaborate on what they are going to do or be. If you have ever been to a high school reunion, you have probably been surprised to find that the people who were so popular and had the most potential are the ones who have achieved very little. By contrast, there are those who were disliked or bullied but who have learned to channel the negative experiences to a positive successful result. As the phrase goes, "Living well is the best revenge." Achieve your dreams and never stop dreaming.

Free Yourself from Time Wasters and Meaningless Distractions

If you are unpopular and disliked, you will save time and energy by not having to jump through the hoops everyone expects you to jump through. You can say no and mean it without worrying what other people think or becoming anchored with the terrible deadweight tasks that no one else wants to do. You can focus on your own career instead of having to save the ass yet again of your lazy colleague in the next cubicle who is earning more than you.

This does not mean you need to be a mean or spiteful person, but rather one living your life with honesty and integrity. By doing this, you will set an example for others and attract sincere people to you. You will often become the person whose opinion everyone respects as you have become a person in tune with your feelings and are successful in all areas of your life.

Now that you have discovered the main advantages of being disliked, live a little. See how many false friends and acquaintances you can weed out of your life by being your authentic self. Chances are, you will never miss them as you move forward to achieve all your goals and dreams.

The Orange Peel Effect: Peeling Back Your Layers

Are You Self-Aware?

If you asked most people if they are self-aware, they will probably say, "Yes." We all like to think that we know ourselves. You know your strengths, weaknesses, and personality type. You understand your thoughts, values, and opinions too, right? For most, not really. The truth is, most of us require a little work on our self-awareness. We are just not as in tune with ourselves as we think we are. Below is a list of surefire signs that you are not as self-aware as you think you are:

Are You Defensive?

When a person feels frightened or scared, they become defensive. Defensiveness is a sign that you're not as self-aware as you might think. Becoming defensive will happen when you do not want to discover something about yourself or during an uncomfortable, difficult situation. It is an attempt on your part to avoid confronting the challenge staring right back at you. The next time you find yourself feeling defensive, take a moment and ask yourself why. What are you trying to avoid by becoming defensive? I used to be very defensive. I did not want to be close to people or talk about my past, so I put up a defensive wall. It worked for me, but others did not see that way. They saw it as me being a total jerk.

Are You Controlling?

Do you suddenly begin to micromanage a situation, trying to control every aspect of the situation? If so, this is a sign that you're avoiding the harsh truth. Or you may begin to evade circumstances that are important to you and your life. In my past, I micromanaged everything. If I could control it, it could not affect me.

Avoidance of Behavior Changes

Beyond being defensive or more controlling, other behavior changes can be a sign that you're not as self-aware as you think. By digging a little deeper, you might find that your behavior changes in other ways. If you are trying to avoid an uncomfortable situation, you may become a reclusive introvert. Or you might become a social butterfly so that you can avoid thinking and being alone with your thoughts. Becoming passive-aggressive, blaming others, or playing the victim are all signs that you're not dealing with something that is important.

These behavior changes and personality traits all come from your attempt at avoidance. If you're avoiding your thoughts, needs, feelings, and opinions, then you're not self-aware. In fact, you are quite the opposite; you're avoiding being self-aware, and that never helps you or anyone else.

Developing Personal Character

Winning Is Contagious

While attending one of my grandson's Little League T-Ball games, I discovered the foundation to why winning is important. At these games, the score is not kept. Although the games are supposed to teach the young players the fundamentals of the game, every player on both teams knew the score. They knew who was winning and who wasn't. The same is true at his soccer games; no score is kept, but every player on both teams knew the score. The young players all knew who had scored the goals or who had made the big hits, and the only ones not keeping score were the coaches. Sitting there at the T-ball games, it struck me as being odd that the only ones not keeping the score were the adults.

I was sitting close to the dugout when my grandson said through the fence, "Grandpa, we are winning!"

"Ethan, nobody is keeping score," I replied

"I know, but we are winning," he said with a big grin on his face.

That's when it hit me; he said the same thing a few weeks prior at his soccer game. That's when I asked myself, "Why is winning so important?" How do five-year-old children know that winning is important enough to keep score? I think it has everything to do with being born with a desire to achieve.

The question becomes, how do you know if you are achieving if you are not keeping score? What bothers me about this idea is if we give everyone a trophy, whether they know they are achieving or not, how do we know the difference between winning and losing? I believe winning is the key to a passionate, productive, and prosperous life. If you are rewarded for both winning and losing with the same level of reward, at some point, the meaning between the two has perished. I believe Vince Lombardi said it best when he stated, "Show me someone who doesn't mind losing and I'll show you a loser." When you devalue winning in your life, you can say goodbye to your untapped talent and potential. When winning is no longer important, the many talents and overwhelming capacity of the human spirit will never surface as a benefit or enable us to experience being our best.

To better understand the concept of the importance of winning, you must understand the definition of winning. The definition of winning is gaining, resulting in or relating to victory in a contest or competition. To put it simply, it is essentially achieving predetermined goals. If you buy into this definition, it is uncomplicated to understand why I say everyone should not receive a trophy. If you win, you have successfully achieved what you set out to do. If you lose, you missed the mark. But falling short of your goal does not make you a failure. Missing the mark means you need to work harder; you need to think differently and take another approach to the challenge. However, if we are rewarded for failing as though we have won, how do we know the difference between winning and losing? Think about it like this: when you win, you succeed; when you lose, you do not.

Why then is winning so important? It's simple. We are all born to win; we are all born to achieve. We all have an inner greatness deep within ourselves that drives a desire to succeed. This desire, this greatness inside each of us is the passion that propels every thought and action we make. That desire is what initiates every moment and interaction of our lives. Have you ever heard anyone say they cannot wait to wake up the next day so they can fail? The answer is more than likely a hard NO! People do not wake up hoping and wishing that they fail; rather, they open their eyes to a world of potential. It's how they act on that potential that will be the deciding factor to their success. What I hear is how tired people are of being less than they can be where they want to go and how much they want more success in their life. Instead of wishing for success, act on your potential and win the day!

The greatest reason why people don't succeed is the lack of believing. If people believed, they would never say they are tired of being less than they can be. They would never let a single thought of losing enter their awareness. People who believe they can win but continuously lose are not changing their potential to win. Rather, day in and day out, they get up in the morning and repeat the same thing they did the day before. They turn off the alarm clock the same way, they use the bathroom the same way, they brush their teeth the same way, they wash their face the same way, they get dressed the same way, and head off to work on the same road every day. Once in the office, they do the same thing they did the day before, right down to what time they get their coffee. They do everything the same way every day. The problem with this is it has become memorized so well that they have become an expert at it. Nothing changed, so there is no reason for their brain to expand. Their life has no reason to change; things are working, so they remain on autopilot. Their brain becomes accustomed to thinking equal to everything they know. So, if they continue to think equal to everything that is familiar to them, the question becomes, "What do they keep creating more of in their life?" THE SAME LIFE!

These individuals keep creating more of the same ideas and processes because of the memorized habits they instilled into their daily routine. To make a difference in your life, you must think greater than what you have become accustomed to. Learn to think greater than yourself. Learn to think greater than the environment that surrounds you. To change, you must create new patterns in your life that will cause your brain to work in new sequences and combinations. Every time you learn something new, you create new pathways and connections in your brain. When you learn, you create new ways to think. When you are living life through memorized processes, you are maintaining old routines and patterns in your brain.

The greatness inside you starts with a vision, an idea that you cannot see, smell, taste, or feel but you know it's there, alive in your mind. It is so alive in you that you begin to live your life as though it is happening now. Therefore we need to know when we are winning and losing. The more we believe we are winning, the more our minds will make the reality of winning seem as though it is taking place now.

Take a moment right now. Wherever you are, whatever you are doing, I want you to stop and take a moment to yourself. Now, intentionally, slow down your mind and consider your thoughts and impulses you are having right now. Quickly, you will realize that all your thoughts and impulses all have to do with completing a cycle of action ending with an achieved goal. When you find the very foundation to this action yielding a result, the goal does not matter. The goal can be as simple as your desire to successfully make it to the grocery store and back home within a time frame, or it can be as complex as developing a business plan and gaining investors. Basically, we are born to achieve goals. That's the bottom line. We as species are goal driven, which has been instilled in us since the beginning of time. The difference between us as humans now and our late cousin, the Cro-Magnon, are the goals have remained the same but have evolved with time. We no longer have survival goals seeking shelter in a cave, hoping we do not become dinner for a sabertooth tiger. Our goals today are more modern and civilized, like trying not to get mauled at the grocery store when you pick up the last bundle of bananas as a soccer mom storms over to let you know that she had her eye on them from across the store. Sorry for her loss, but you achieved the goal of obtaining the last bundle of bananas, and she did not.

Winning plays a vital role in who we are as individuals. When losing is an acceptable outcome, you are turning your back on your birth-given talents to achieve your personal greatness. Your highest and most honorable life obligation is to be a winner. It's as if the deep desire of winning we all have inside of us is a black hole longing to be filled. It is that black hole where we sense a missing link in our lives but remain unaware of what this feeling is. You may have tried to fill this emptiness with material items, thinking it will quench your thirst for achievement. Material items seldom do, but when we win, the feeling of achievement cannot be replaced. Winning creates a legacy in our life. When you establish a life of personal wins, over time, they build on each other, and each success snowballs to the point where winning becomes the avalanche you need in your life rather than the exception.

I believe the most important reason for becoming a winner is how it defines you as a person. It is what it says about who you are and how you live your life. It is what your desires and aspirations become. It sets the example of "If you can do it, so can I." Each of your successes have a direct impact on others by revealing to them that living a successful, productive life is possible for anyone when the right steps are taken to achieve your desired goals. The bottom line is, winning makes it completely clear that life is a privilege, not an entitlement. That correlates with the understanding of why everyone should not receive a trophy. When they do, the opposite occurs where life becomes an entitlement, not a privilege. Whether its competing in sports or building a new business, I would rather have a team overwhelmed with a desire to win than have a team stacked with talented individuals who care less whether they win or lose so long as they receiver their paycheck.

To win, we must maintain the body and mind we were given. I know you probably think that sounds strange, but without a well-kept mind and body, we don't win. We can only be as good as our mind and body allows. If you are not getting enough sleep, the right things to eat, or enough exercise, both mentally and physically, you are unable to win. When we properly maintain our mind and body, we enable our full capacity to win consistently.

Being optimistic is a key ingredient to winning and in developing a vision for a better future. Some say you must fail to move forward; however, I also believe the same is true with winning. To win and achieve in life, you must fail first. When you fail, you learn the necessary lesson from the given scenario that enables you to move forward. Each time you fail, you inch closer to winning. Several years ago, I was fortunate to play a role in the development of a new high school football program. Out of the initial twenty-nine players who were present at the first practice, only six players had ever stepped on a football field before. The first season was a learning experience as this team only won a single game. Once we finished the season, the players hit the weight room and became stronger by putting in the necessary work needed to succeed. Although we only won two games in the second season, the players continued to put in the hard work needed to get better. Our third season was plagued with multiple distractions. The first three weeks of the season was delayed due to multiple hurricanes. As a result, we managed to win four games. Each year, the players learned from their mistakes made during the previous year. In our fourth year, we went undefeated and played in the state playoffs. Desire and optimism are keys to winning, but desire is what keeps you moving forward after you lose. The key to the victories you long for is directly linked to how deep your desire is to win. When you have desire, you can learn to win; and better yet, you can learn how to become a consistent winner.

The Importance of Setting Priorities

When we are overwhelmed with tasks at work, we tend to believe that we are achieving success. From personal experience, I have concluded that busy work does not yield productivity. Yes, I have spun my wheels many times thinking I was moving up the success ladder; but in the end, all I was creating was an environment that didn't allow me to move forward. I was inundated with unnecessary unimportant tasks that kept me in my place, STUCK. Something to keep in mind is that activity does not always yield accomplishment. To move beyond this, you must prioritize your tasks according to importance. When you prioritize, you should be continually thinking ahead, to know what is important, to know what's next so you may adjust accordingly. Prioritizing tasks enables you to understand how everything relates to the overall success of your plan. When you prioritize, you must ask yourself three simple questions. Don't sugarcoat your answers. Be brutally honest with yourself. When you decide to prioritize your life and ask yourself these questions, your life will change immediately! Ask yourself the following:

1. What is *required*?
    a. What do you need to address immediately that nobody else can or should do for you?

2. What gives me the greatest **return on invested time**?
   a. Work in your areas of greatest strength! Think about the things you're doing that can be done 80 percent as well by someone else. Don't be afraid to delegate time-consuming tasks that others can manage.

3. What yields the greatest **reward**?
   a. This question is not about money. Life is too short to not do the things you enjoy and love. When considering this question, think about what energizes you and keeps you passionate about what you do.

Every day, you should be thinking, "Today, I am giving my time only to the things that pass the REQUIREMENT, RETURN, and REWARD TEST." If you do this every day, you will start your day off right. No longer will you feel like you are spinning your wheels. You will feel a sense of accomplishment as your activity will equal your productivity.

What I know is this: ***Successful people never advance to a point where they no longer need to prioritize.*** Prioritization is something successful people continuously do, whether they're leading billion-dollar corporations or local little league baseball organizations. There are many reasons people do not prioritize. When you are busy, you believe you are achieving. WRONG! Remember, being busy does not yield production. Another reason is that it requires people to think ahead, to know what's important, to know what's coming next, to see how it relates, and THAT ALL TAKES HARD WORK. Not everyone enjoys working hard, but when you do the changes you want, your life begins to happen. Ultimately, prioritizing forces us to step out of our comfort zone, enabling us to perform at a higher level. For some, stepping out of our comfort zone is downright painful but a necessary act that is a requirement for success.

Some time ago, I was on a cruise with my wife, sister-in-law, and brother-in-law. As some of you may know, on cruise ships, they typically have silent art auction where people can place a bid and purchase different works. I enjoy collecting art and can remember the moment as I walked down one of the ship's hallways, passing the many works hanging from the walls. One of the artists whose works I enjoy collecting the most is Scott Jacobs. As I walked down this hallway full of art, I found two of his pieces. Without reserve, I placed my bid in hopes that I would be lucky enough to win. Success!

A short while after the cruise, my sister-in-law and brother-in-law came to visit, and I showed them the two pictures hanging in my office. My brother-in-law asked, "If your house was on fire and you could save only one of the pictures, which one would you choose?" After struggling to find the answer, I told him, "I would save both after I save my wedding pictures, but only if I had already saved the pictures of my children and grandchildren." I explained to him, "It's all about priorities, man." As life presses on, you will begin to discover that some items and actions hold a higher priority than others. Which has higher priority, your job or your family? I hope this is not a hard question for you to answer. If you use the three-simple questions I asked earlier, it becomes simple:

1. *What is required?*
2. *What gives me the greatest return?*
3. *What brings me the greatest reward?*

One of the ways I found that helps me keep my priorities in line is called the Pareto principle. This is a principle that is based off this simple guideline: *if you focus your attention on the activities that rank in the top 20 percent in terms of importance, you have an 80 percent return on your effort.* In other words, if you have one hundred customers, the top twenty customers will provide you 80 percent of your business, so focus on them. Simple, right?

John Wooden, former UCLA basketball coach and author of a bestselling book *Pyramid of Success*, sets a great example as to why priorities are important if you want to be successful. Coach Wooden was the most winningest college basketball coach of all time. He coached his players on the importance of priorities and planned his team's practices meticulously based on the important tasks. Time was not wasted in practice, and at any given moment, all members of the team were involved and expected to remain focused. Wooden's planning started at the beginning of each season, when he would begin to identify the team's priorities for the New Year. These priorities were based on the team's previous year's experiences and accomplishments. This high-level prioritization would then feed into the day-to-day planning of team practices. One of his greatest strengths as a coach was his ability to design practices that would address several priority areas simultaneously.

Coach Wooden's direct focus was on development of his players on the court and in the classroom so they may reach their maximum potential. "It was never his goal to win championships or even to beat the other team but to get each person to play to his potential." In forty years of coaching, Coach Wooden had only one losing season, his first. Over the course of his career, as a head basketball coach, his teams won ten national championships along with four unbeaten seasons.

Another example of the importance of setting priorities can be seen in 1981, during the transition of leadership at General Electric. Jack Welch took over the leadership of GE in 1981, when the company was doing very well. During this time, GE was the eleventh largest company on the stock market and highly diversified with 350 business units. Welch decided that the company was not reaching its full potential and had a vision to become greater. He decided that to move forward, GE needed to downsize the amount of business units currently under their conglomerate umbrella. He had one criterion for deciding whether to keep a business unit or not: Can it be first or second in its market worldwide? For 348 of the 350 units, the answer was no. Welch closed or sold off 348 businesses/product lines, raising $10 billion. He then spent $17 billion on new acquisitions and an additional $18 billion in investment in the remaining parts of the original company. By 1989, GE had only fourteen core businesses, but each of them was either first or second in its worldwide market.

Because of Jack's leadership, the stock price of General Electric grew from $4 a share in 1981 to $103.62 a share in May of 1983 and then in June of 1983 the stock split two for one. In two years, GE went from eleventh on the stock exchange to the most valuable company in the world.

1. *Are you spread out over many units like GE prior to Jack Welch taking charge?*

OR

2. *Are you focused on the few things that bring the highest rewards in your life like Coach Wooden?*

You will never advance if you do not prioritize, and you will never advance to a point where you no longer need to prioritize. Why is it that after a week or a month or even a year passes, you feel frustrated by the things that are left undone? Why do you think it is that the actions you SHOULD have done were not and the things that you SHOULD NOT have done were?

NO PRIORITY!

We spend our time in the ways we choose, and there is nothing we do without choosing. You are correct in assuming our choices are not always deliberate or visible. You have a choice to work or not to work, to cut your grass or not cut your grass, to take a phone call or to wait. Every choice you make is based on the reward you believe you will receive. If you did not receive a reward from your actions, chances are you will not continue the behavior. When you learn to prioritize, you learn to do the things that matter most and give you the greatest rewards. If this is the case, WHY WOULD YOU NOT PRIORITIZE YOUR LIFE?

When you prioritize, you change from being reactive in nature to a proactive leader. Instead of handling the results of a "cause and effect" situation, prioritizing will actively select the things that will receive your focus and attention. Priorities enable you to become proactive by leading your focus to what is important.

Dale Carnegie, an American writer and public speaker, told a story about two men who were out chopping wood. One man worked hard all day, took no breaks, and only stopped briefly for lunch. The other man took several breaks during the day and a short nap at lunch. At the end of the day, the woodsman who had taken no breaks was quite disturbed to see that the other man had cut more wood than he did. He said, "I don't understand. Every time I looked around, you were sitting down, yet you cut more wood than I did." His companion asked, "Did you also notice that while I was sitting down, I was sharpening my ax?" Setting priorities enables you to take the time to sharpen your own axe that is needed to chop more wood in less time. Without setting priorities, you become more reactive as you respond to the day's events as they occur. Without priorities, you will spend more time chopping wood while yielding the same result as the man who sharpens his axe. This prevents you from obtaining the greatest return and rewards. It is NOT a lack of time that is the issue but a problem of setting PRIORITIES.

When you don't set your own priorities, you live a life pursuing other priorities set by someone else. You navigate through life based on what is important to your boss, your parents, your children, or even society in general. When you live this lifestyle, your days become filled with tasks for others and to-do lists that keeps your head spinning around the clock. You become so busy for other people that you might find it hard to sleep at night, exercise, plan a trip, or work on personal relationships. With this approach, you find yourself spending much time focusing every ounce of your energy and attention on things that, in the end, have minor significance. These are things that do not add to the fulfillment of your own scope of life. When you think about it, it is a sad way to spend your life as you are focused on fulfilling other's needs.

If spending time with your family is important to you, make it a priority. Make the conscious effort to do so by taking the action necessary to make it happen. When you just say it or think about it, you may never find the time to make it happen. Prioritize your days by scheduling fun activities for the whole family; create the family rituals and do things with your family on a regular basis. My family is my priority. It has always been and always will be. Have I missed football games, track meets, volleyball games? YES! Life happens, and I make no excuses for those times I missed an event. Instead, I work harder at prioritizing my time and what is important to me so that I will not miss the things that mean the most to me.

There is no other activity that will impact the direction of your life more than setting priorities. You can have all the determination it takes, all the discipline you can muster up, all the motivation and inspiration you can bring to bear, but if your efforts are scattered or misdirected, you will have insignificant impact on whatever it is you are trying to achieve. Priorities provides clarity to all the many possible directions life will try to take you. Without priorities, you will often find yourself falling short of your goals and ambitions. We fall short, not because we are incapable, but rather we have made something else more important. This something else can be a job, a TV show, yard work, your social life, or your family. None of these scenarios are negative, but it does become apparent how important they become when you consciously look at your priorities and decide what truly is important and what is not. For those who believe everything is significant and believe it is impossible to prioritize when everything is important, I suggest this: *if everything is of equal importance, you must decide by using the three questions I gave you earlier.*

It is time to buckle up, strap yourself in, and become serious on what matters most by setting your priorities. This will require hard work and effort. The task of prioritizing your life is difficult and at times may seem overwhelming. But once you decide what's important, the journey we all call life begins to smooth out and become easier. The pilot in your life might even turn off the seatbelt sign. Once you really understand what is required of you, you will be able to make the right decisions for the direction you want your life to take. If you want your life to take a different path, set the GPS on a new destination by setting the right priorities first. Remember, it is easy to be busy cranking out the things on your to-do list that are worthless. Find worth and do the tasks that are far more difficult to choose. Do the important things based on the priorities you set forth.

Are You Living a Lie?

Unless we love the truth, we cannot know it.
—Blaise Pascal

Here's a quick quiz for you. Answer the questions honestly.
Do you feel

- *like you are constantly hiding behind a mask?*
- *worried that others will not like you?*
- *that if you say no, you are a bad person and will let everyone down?*
- *trapped in a life that does not seem to be your own?*
- *like you are always comparing yourself to others, with them on top and you on the bottom?*
- *as if you're finding yourself not good enough, no matter how hard you try?*
- *afraid that if your boss, coworkers, spouse. or children found out X about you, they would never look at you in the same way again?*

If you answered yes to any of these questions, then the likely truth is that you are living unauthentically. But you are not alone.

Living an unauthentic life, a lie, is an easy trap to fall into. which is why so many of us are trapped there. As you try to climb out, you feel as if you are in quicksand. The harder you try, the deeper you sink, and the more difficult it becomes. However, the effort put forth can be well worth it if the result is a happier, healthier you. It seems as if almost from the moment we are born, we have a certain role in the family with a certain set of expectations both spoken and unspoken. Our family and the wider world are telling us who we are supposed to be rather than allowing us to express who we truly are. Our parents want us to be happy, but we might not have within us what it takes to be a doctor or lawyer, get accepted to their prestigious alma mater, or follow in their career footsteps. On the other hand, our parents might have low expectations for us; maybe there has never been a college graduate in the family, or they got by working in a convenience store all their lives, which they believe should be good enough for you too. We receive a range of messages about how we are supposed to perform, think, and be. Society tells us that children should be seen and not heard, we must never waste food, we should always clean our plates. Over time, these habits become second nature to us; however, they are not necessarily healthy or helpful if they lead to being terrified of speaking in public or being vastly overweight.

When we go to school, we might have a teacher who is never satisfied no matter how hard we work. Or we might be told we are not good at (you fill in the blank), and so we should not even bother to try. To this day, fifty-some years later, I can still remember the moment in seventh grade when a coach told me loud and clear in front of a gym full of my peers that I didn't make the team. He reinforced this rejection by letting me and everyone there know that I was too small, too slow, and would probably never amount to anything. We might be bullied over the way we look, dress, speak, or even for being too smart or too stupid at school. Growing up on Long Island in New York, I was bullied until my family moved to Florida, where I entered junior high school. I was bullied for being too smart, wearing glasses, being a Boy Scout, and for many other reasons that, to this day, I don't fully understand. Every day after school, I had to fight my way home, facing off with a group of three to five people around my age. Then my parents moved us to Florida, where I grew up physically becoming one of big kids on the block. My life changed for the better in ways I could have never imagined and in ways that still amaze me to this day.

Rather than receiving encouragement or support from the adults who influence our lives, we are told to "man up" or be more "ladylike." There are now more opportunities for both men and women to defy traditional expectations, but the truth is that we often internalize various unhelpful attitudes and actions as normal and therefore judge ourselves as abnormal or less than perfect if we wish to live our lives differently. Peer pressure and parental pressure can build in us, resulting in our mind constructing a false mask of the "perfect" child, sibling, spouse, and so on. As the pressure builds from outside to conform, your own authentic self begins to feel trapped and miserable, like a caged tiger pacing back and forth, longing to be set free.

If you have been living a lie to please others, you owe it to yourself to start living a more authentic life in which your true self can shine through.

Your Authentic Signature

Truth is incontrovertible. Panic may resent it, ignorance may deride it, malice may distort it, but there it is.
—Winston Churchill

Being yourself is self-explanatory. Most days. do you wake up and do what you want to do? Do you avoid following the crowds? Do you get out of bed without the fear of judgement? Unfortunately, for many, this is not the way the world works as most of us try to avoid being our authentic selves so we may fit in the status quo. Many of us do this without even realizing it. It might seem insignificant, but when you ponder this notion of going with the status quo, do you feel as if you have become a robot? When we avoid being our authentic self, we become the robot that others want us to be while suppressing our own creativity, ingenuity, and self-awareness.

Oh no! You did it again. You just said yes to another favor for a friend even though it will totally inconvenience you. Or you have been "volunteered" again by your colleagues for a local fundraiser, even though you are overwhelmed with tasks filling up your plate as your stress level rises and your hours of sleep diminishes. If you are finding yourself becoming the "yes" man or "yes" woman when you should be saying no, you are not living faithfully to your authentic self. There is new research coming out about the mind and body connection. The research explores how our moods and emotions affect our health and how our health affects our moods and emotions. Many people have an increased interest in how living authentically can improve mind, body, and spirit, helping to create a happier self.

When people ask you "Who are you?" How do you answer? Do you answer with, "I'm a dad," "I'm a mom," "I'm a brother," "I'm a businessman?" We all have different variations and characterizations that define who we are that we use in different situations. You might act one way in front of your friends, another way in front of your clients, and yet another way in front your significant other. Those "invented selves" are normal, and it is something we all do. Where we get in trouble is when we do it and it is not truthful. Defining your authentic self is difficult, especially these days where it means as much when you are in person as it does in the way you present yourself online in social media. However, that is not what being authentic is all about. It is not about expressing your opinions without filter; rather, it has everything to do with confidently knowing what those opinions are.

For some, the idea of the authentic self may sound like new age nonsense, but an increasing body of evidence from organizations like the American Psychological Association has shown the impact of stress, obesity, heart disease. and more on our psychological well-being, and vice versa. Your moods can dramatically affect your health without you even realizing it. Depression and anxiety can prevent you from leading a full and normal life.

To better understand your authentic self, you need to first understand what authentic means. *Webster* defines it as

- not false or copied; genuine; real: an authentic antique.
- having the origin supported by unquestionable evidence; authenticated; verified.
- entitled to acceptance or belief because of agreement with known facts or experience; reliable; trustworthy.
- The key words used should POP right out at you:
- Not false—in other words, being true and truthful
- Not copied—in other words, being original and unique
- Genuine
- Real
- Authenticated
- Verified

- Entitled to acceptance
- Entitled to belief or credence
- Believable due to known facts and experience
- Reliable

Being an authentic person is being someone who is real, not fake, and all your words and actions verify who you are. Your actions back up your words, and your words are backed up by your actions. By being genuine, authentic, and reliable, you will gain acceptance from others and obtain their confidence in you. People will begin to trust and believe in you as the facts and experiences they have with you confirm who you are. Your sense of worth will begin to grow with them. You are a person of integrity, an honest person, with morals and scruples. You are a complete person guided by strong ethics rather than one who changes with every passing moment.

Your level of trustworthiness and credibility is vital for both your business and personal life. If you are genuine and reliable, people will believe in you, and doors of opportunities will begin to open. In your personal life, your relationships will flourish as happiness pumps through your veins with every heartbeat. People in your life will feel confident in the person you have become and begin to feel more comfortable when working with you.

The necessity of being real and genuine can and will get you far, but honesty is a requirement we all must embrace. Being honest about your feelings by not suppressing them or expressing them inappropriately is vital for self-growth. Exploding in anger or frustration when situations do not go as planned will destroy your authenticity. Living an authentic life allows you to respond to others in an open and honest manner without being defensive, offensive, or abusive. When situations yield the outcome we do not desire, we should not be throwing a fit that resembles a three-year-old child having our toy taken from us. We yell, scream, cry, and throw things until the other party gives us what we want. On the other hand, you can express your emotions in a healthy way, which is an odd concept for some—but necessary. When we express healthy emotions to a given situation, we speak from the heart about our likes, dislikes, and innermost desires.

Living an authentic life is also about knowing who you are, which by this point has been addressed from the self-reflection chapter in previous chapters. This authenticity is about embracing every aspect of yourself including the skeletons in your closet that you are ashamed of or the fear you hold when thinking others might find out what you have hidden deep within. You fear that if people know your inner being, they may disown you as a friend, family, member or colleague.

When you live an authentic life,

- you know your strengths and weaknesses and act accordingly.
- you recognize your imperfections.
- you own your mistakes, learn from them, and push forward.
- you look for opportunities to let your true self rise to the surface.
- you invest time in yourself remaining balanced and whole.

Do you have an anger issue? Maybe, maybe not. But if you happen to fly off the handle at any given moment, addressing this characteristic through an anger management course is an action of an individual accepting the fact that they have a problem. Acknowledging your anger-control issues and acting to correct it is the correct course of action when living a more authentic life. Such a person understands that their anger is a weakness that affects all their relationships in a negative way and will be harmful to the people around them if left unchecked. To be their best self, they must recognize the anger, find the trigger mechanism, and accept the problem they have with anger so they can move forward in a positive way. "But what if anger is a part of my authentic self?" says the lonely person with nothing to show.

Anger may be a part of who you are, but many of us have negative characteristics we need to improve. No one is perfect, and all of us have aspects in our personality that we need to improve. However, instead of investing the time needed to work through our issues, we hide them, we bury them, we ignore them. Even worse, we become actors, playing roles that allow us to hide the things we like least about ourselves. Why? It's much easier to do than facing the issues. Whether you realize it or not, this type of façade affects all aspects of your life. It is hard to live authentically in a world where appearance is everything and being fake or a fraud gains you greater rewards than being genuine. For what seem to be very valid reasons, many of us do not live authentically.

Who does not love being popular and having lots of friends, family, a great romantic relationship, and so on? We see this popularity on the TV, in the movies, at work, and some of us have a great desire for it and are willing to do anything to get it. We long for the harmonious relations with everyone around us as we avoid the stress and strife that hurt our inner being. We want great connections with our loved ones and the intimacy that society says is associated with marriage, but if you look at the divorce rate in our country, the numbers are astonishing. Studies show that most people do not live authentically. The romantic phase of a relationship usually only lasts from eight to eighteen months. During this phase, we tend to view everything with rose-colored glasses, long walks on the beach, bubble baths by candlelight; but as time presses on, the cute little laugh we found adorable now sounds like fingernails on a blackboard as the reality of life sets in.

Studies show that most marriages end in divorce due to arguments that stem from financial hardships. Yet how many couples take the time and trouble to sit down to discuss their finances and hidden secrets they may have. How many do you think discuss past bankruptcies or hidden accounts? Most do not. After speaking with many young couples, I have found that most of them have separate checking and saving accounts, splitting the bills fifty-fifty each month. I find this astonishing. Doesn't a marriage mean both parties become one? Yet many couples are not willing to combine their assets. They believe "this is my money that I earned, that is money she earned, and I deserve to spend my money the way I want." Is this marriage? Yes. But is it an authentic unity? That's for you to decide.

Another common cause of marital breakup is infidelity. The cheating partner will usually find a range of excuses and justifications for what they have done. The truth is, they are not living an authentic life. "I love the way they make me feel," or "I can be honest with them," says the person tearing your heart out. How much honesty is involved in sneaking around and pretending to be single by taking off your wedding ring as you order the next round at the bar for the beautiful woman sitting beside you? The point is, no matter how we move, how we sit, or how we stand, we will always be uncomfortable. You will never be comfortable if you are dishonest with yourself and others.

Even if you haven't been on either side of these types of situations, deceiver or deceived, chances are, you have friends or family who have experienced them. Do not fool yourself; we have all deceived someone at some point in our lives for a positive or negative outcome. "Does this pair of pants make me look fat?" "You don't mind watching my baby for an hour, do you?" All the while knowing the answer to these questions are not always the ones they want to hear.

At work, have you ever become boastful as you brag about how awesome you are? We all do it from time to time to make ourselves look better than we are. When you hold things back from your loved ones, you become inauthentic. We hold things back in fear of the reaction that might occur when we tell it like it is. Or you don't share your entire self with the person you are dating because you are concerned they might discover the skeletons in your closet that will end the relationship. Or you don't tell your spouse the truth to either protect their feelings or "save face" by not admitting your mistakes. To remain popular, we avoid rocking the boat, we avoid saying the ugly truth, or we avoid telling people no. We swallow our disappointment because we have been taught that being negative is a result of insecurity. One of my favorite examples comes from a statement I heard many times. "You should never appear ungrateful or unladylike or, if you are a man, too emotional." Growing up, many of us as children were taught that we should be seen, not heard. This resembles obedience if the child complies, but it also leads to a loss of voice from the individual. If you are a parent, allowing your child to express themselves is key to their development. Allow your children the autonomy to expression as they need to be heard just as much as be seen. We all have a voice that should be heard. All these examples are a result of our fear in what might happen if we are honest with ourselves or others.

Inauthentic lifestyle characteristics:

- You are attempting to be someone you are not.
- You are lying about your feelings and emotions.
- You are lying about your accomplishments.
- You lack energy because you are always putting on a front for people.
  - The happy smiling face when you are miserable.
  - Stiff upper lip despite being very upset.

- The number of conflicts in your work or personal life grow.
- Stress elevates like a pressure cooker getting ready to explode.
- You lose respect from others as they begin to believe you are false or insincere.

If you recognize any of these signs in your own life, it is time for a change. Time to work on returning to your authentic self and being faithful to it. It is time to be honest with your reality.

There are many emotional and physical consequences of living an inauthentic life. One of the reasons people lie is they fear the consequences that will result from telling the truth. Often, it is the lie, not being authentic, that makes a terrible situation worse. Being dishonest will cause the consequences to worsen as you try to avoid the initial repercussions. When you are living behind a tapestry of lies, covering up secrets, or trying to duck your way out of the consequences of your actions, you are living an inauthentic life.

You may think you are in the clear, that your lies are safe, but there are also many emotional consequences of living an inauthentic life.

- Feelings of being unappreciated, unloved, or undervalued for who you are
- Feelings of not "being good enough" to be yourself
- Feelings of fraud and undeserving of good fortune
- Thinking you must keep people happy or fulfill certain expectations

Emotional consequences will be accompanied by physical changes such as the following:

- Stress
- Anxiety
- High blood pressure
- Headaches
- Backache
- Decreased immunity to fight illnesses

Even armed with the knowledge of emotional and physical consequences, you may still be resisting the idea of allowing yourself to live more authentically.

What are you afraid of?

- The discomfort of showing your emotions
- Inability to express your emotions in a positive or constructive way
- Unable to feel and associate emotions to give a proper response
- Fear of showing weakness
- Having to learn how to integrate your emotions

The truth is, you will never be comfortable being numb or suppressing your emotions. Some people will turn to external remedies such as drinking, drug addiction, or sexual excess all in attempts to numb their emotions. Ironically, often, this will cause them to feel far worse than the feelings they are trying to hide. Possibly, the reasons you have become inauthentic with yourself is that you feel it is easier to stick with the tried and tested instead of stepping out of your comfort zone. There are three reasons for feeling this way. The first and most obvious reason is the fear of change. Second, you develop a fear that people will not approve of the changes you are making. Third, you feel as though you are a fraud on so many levels that it has become difficult to distinguish a starting point for your desired change to living an authentic life.

It is important to deal with your feelings and with your situation as it is now. You are unable to change the past, but you can take your experiences and learn from them. There are many lessons that can be learned from your past that can help you improve your future.

- Start by expressing yourself
- Start by accepting your imperfections
- Start by sharing your burdens
- Start by looking forward, not back
- Start by facing your inner truth
- Start by learning to say no
- Start by asking for help

If you are unable to make the changes you desire on your own, seek help by talking to a professional. For some, deep traumas such as abuse, neglect, or posttraumatic stress disorder has a greater impact on their life. You may not even realize that these traumas are holding you back until you begin the journey toward discovering your authentic self.

You owe it to yourself to be the best you can be, so do not let fear hold you back from being your true self. Once you begin, you will be surprised at all the positive changes that will occur in your day-to-day routines. You will start to feel more relaxed, less stressed, and you will take pleasure in the better things in your life. Your relationships at home and in the office will seem easier and more fulfilling as a sense of being productive will consume you. As you continue to accomplish your goals, you will in turn become more confident. Learning how to say no will keep you focused on your own goals rather than living in service to the agendas of others. Finally, you will discover that the ability to express emotions—whether it be joy or sorrow, fear or courage—does not make you weak. It strengthens you in your own eyes and in the eyes of others as you live your life on your terms without trying to hide your authentic self.

Stop Complaining! Be Thankful Every Day

When you rise in the morning, give thanks for the light, for your life, for your strength. Give thanks for your food and for the joy of living. If you see no reason to give thanks, the fault lies in yourself.
—Tecumseh

When life has you down, it is helpful to reflect on the many things that make you thankful. Each of us are thankful for different reasons and different things, just as there are as many different reasons and things that bring us down. Whether what's bringing you down is that you cannot buy the new car you want or that you don't know where your next meal is coming from, there are reasons to be thankful. For many individuals, there is no doubt life has dealt them a lousy poker hand that dominates their life.

What we believe we experience in life is based on our perspective of life's reality. If this is true, it is easy to see how we can change an unfortunate negative situation to a positive fulfilling life of possibilities. Rather than struggling with thoughts of never getting what you want, change your perspective to being thankful for what life has already provided.

Sure, it is easy to allow negative people to influence your life and steal your energy. Negative people steal your energy and increase their power over you. When your energy is drained, it becomes difficult to remain positive, which is even more reason to understand what you are truly thankful for. When you understand what you are thankful for, the negative issues and negative people become insignificant.

What are you thankful for? Very simple question but, for some, very difficult to answer. Some answers may even be cliché. But after speaking with many different people, it seems not so much. On the surface, the question is simple; but for those I have spoken with, it is a difficult and many times a complicated question to answer. I found, through asking this question, many people are overwhelmed with complaining rather than considering the good things life has provided.

Spending time constantly rehashing past mistakes is time wasted. Those mistakes are in the past, but if allowed, they will drive negativity in the present. Certainly, we can learn from our past mistakes, but that should be it as we learn to move forward. We all have experienced events and circumstances in life that challenge us to our very soul. Our limits are constantly tested by the people in our lives, by those who teach us, by those who guide us, by those in our family, by adversity, and by our health. What we do when our limit is reached makes the difference in how we live our lives, positively or negatively.

I am thankful for my family. They keep me centered and provide purpose in my life. My family has played a role in shaping me into who I am today. When I am with my family, I do not need much more. I am thankful for my health, which enables me to enjoy the many things life has to offer such as time spent with my family. With good health, I can work and provide for my family. Most importantly, I am thankful for today and every day I wake up to a new day. Regardless of what has me down, I can always be thankful for my life today, my family, and my health.

Attitude Is Everything

Attitude will make all the difference in anything you do. From personal experience, I can tell you ATTITUDE is everything. Positive attitudes win, and negative attitudes lose. You might think differently, but for me, there hasn't been a time in my life where anything ever turned out positive when I attacked the situation with a negative attitude. In fact, I can't recall a time ever in my life when a negative attitude won anything. Looking back, all a negative attitude ever awarded me was trouble—and sometimes, a great deal of trouble. It reminds me of when I used to coach youth sports and I would hear, "I hate practice!" "This sucks!" "Why are we doing this?" I would always ask the athlete who I thought said it, "Then why are you here?" One negative attitude on a team can bring the entire team down, especially if the team leader is the one with the bad attitude. It is true that attitudes are contagious. I would tell fellow coaches, "I would rather have a team full of average athletes with strong, positive attitudes than a team full of superstars with poor negative attitudes."

When I was in the military, attitude was everything. In some cases, a negative attitude led to injury or even death. At least if you had a positive attitude, you had a fighting chance to prevail or overcome. I have always viewed a negative attitude as giving up before you ever get started. Looking back, I remember with my children, each one of them at some point had a moment in their high school sports careers where they questioned their abilities to remain a part of whatever team they were on. I would tell them that's not an attitude that wins. I would tell them, "Close your eyes, imagine your hands are palms up, about shoulder-width apart, and that you have a yardstick lying across your hands. Now imagine you are looking at the number 18, which is the middle of the yardstick. Consider the middle as your starting point, 1 as the most negative attitude you could have, and 36 as the best positive attitude you could have. When you start anything with a positive attitude, you are at 18 and only have half the way to go to be at your best positive attitude, a real winner. Anything less than 18 and look at how much farther you must go to be a winner. It gave them a way to picture where they were and how far they had to go with regard to their attitude. It showed them how a negative attitude set them back from their goals. A negative attitude works hard at keeping you from reaching success, from achieving the win.

Attitude is your set of emotions, beliefs, and behaviors that you have toward a person, an object, a thing, or even an event. Studies have shown that the attitudes you have toward whatever it is are primarily the results of your life experiences and upbringing. There is no doubt attitude has a powerful influence over your behavior. The good news is, even though attitudes are enduring, they are a product of your experiences, which means they are learned, which means they CAN BE CHANGED. When I think of examples of how attitude can change the game, the 2013 Sugar Bowl game between Florida and Louisville comes to mind.

This game demonstrates that when capabilities are very similar, many times, the deciding factor will be who has the better attitude behind a winning belief. Not even ten minutes into the opening quarter of the game, the twenty-first-ranked Louisville team was up 14–0 over the third ranked Florida Gators. The second half of the game started with Florida kicking off to Louisville. Florida kicked an onside kick, a risky move they had not done all season. The Florida coaches must have assumed that Louisville had prepared for the game based on what they had seen on this season's game films. Since there were no onside kicks on any of the game films, maybe Louisville would be caught by surprise; however, that was not the case. In fact, Louisville had anticipated the possibility and had mostly wide receivers on the field instead of the special team players, which was something the Florida coaches completely missed. Louisville recovered the onside kick, which was the true turning point in the game. When the TV camera panned along the Florida bench and then to the head coach, it was visibly obvious their attitude toward winning shifted. In the end Louisville, ranked twenty-first, pulled off a stunning upset defeat of the number 3–ranked Florida Gators. Attitudes drive beliefs. A positive attitude drives a "We can win" belief.

There are many stories of how a positive attitude won out in the end. Just before the German Lutheran pastor Dietrich Bonhoeffer was executed by the Nazis, he said, "You can't do away with my right to choose my attitude toward my circumstances." Or how about UCLA professor of medical humanities Norman Cousins, who often reminded his medical students at UCLA that "the control center of your life is your attitude." Do not misinterpret me as I still believe it is possible to achieve success without a good attitude. But attitude will determine how much you enjoy the success you achieve. Sigmund Freud wrote groundbreaking books and was considered a genius during his lifetime BUT from the time he was a teenager, he was pessimistic, skeptical, and often a very depressed individual.

Even though it is possible for people with audacious talent but a poor attitude to achieve great accomplishments, it does not happen very often. When it does, it requires incredible amounts of effort and hardships. The bottom line is, people with undesirable attitudes may achieve success at some point in their life, but they do not get very far in life. We all know someone that fits the mold. Hopefully, you are not one of them. If you are, you have self-reflection work you need to complete. Throughout time, we repeatedly see people who are barely average and are motivated to achieve great things. When their attitudes are adjusted to be more positive, they can channel their energy in the right way, enabling them to accomplish their goals. The key ingredient is attitude—not aptitude—that will determine the altitude of your life. The skills you acquire in life do not entitle you to achieve. The intelligence that you may have does not mean you will become successful. Only your attitude will determine your future and how you will get there. How far are you willing to go? How will you change your attitude in a positive way? How much will you make of what has been handed to you?

When you start a new assignment or task, it is your attitude that determines how much you will invest into it. If this is true, you have only two choices: start whatever it is with a positive attitude, ready to see it through; or begin with a negative attitude, not caring if you even get started. I would often tell the young people I coached not to think of it as "All is well that ends well" rather think of it as "All is well that begins well."

There are many important tasks in life that must be done; however, we do not take the time to relish in the thought of acting when it comes to those tasks. What I have found that corrects my thoughts is to fixate my mind on the facts, not on my feelings. I work diligently on focusing on the possibilities rather than the problems. By doing so, this allows me to maintain a positive attitude. A few years ago, I heard a story about a mother and her daughter who went shopping. While shopping, the daughter noticed that every store they went into, her mother complained about everything—you name it, and she complained about it. The crowds, the articles of clothing not on sale, the music playing in the speakers, the awful smell and strong perfumes while entering the stores, and the obnoxious style of clothing of today's youth are just a few of the many complaints she wanted everyone to know about. In the last store they went into, the mom had a heated argument with a clerk. There was no blood shed during this argument between the two, but when the exchange ended, the mom turned to her daughter and said, "I am never coming back to this store again. Did you see that dirty look she gave me?" Filled with annoyance and out of patience, the daughter responded, "She did not give it to you, Mom. You had the terrible attitude and dirty look when you came into the store."

You see, our attitudes set the tone on how we interact with others and how people respond and interact with us. If you want to have positive, fulfilling interactions with people, treat others the way you want to be treated. If you maintain a negative outlook and constantly complain about what is wrong in the situation rather than the positive, you may miss the rewards that you desire deep within. In the situation above, the mother focused her energy on the negative external factors she could not control rather than enjoying the rewards of spending quality time with her daughter.

With so many technological advances and the spread of social media, everyone is becoming more competitive, looking for something they can take advantage of to help get them to the top of the ladder. We become specialized through our training, we acquire advanced degrees, we spend many hours in the gym and do everything in our power to advance in our profession. But with all advantages being similar, your attitude is what wins. It is also true that even when nothing is equal, it will be your attitude that still wins. Consider your positive attitude and character becoming your own secret weapon that wins the war. With a positive attitude, the sense of achievement becomes an addictive drug that you continue to want and work for. Remember, it is your attitude, not your achievements that bring you happiness as you can still have achievement without a positive outlook. Happiness has an intimate relationship with a positive attitude.

Eighteenth-century poet Samuel Johnson explained attitude and contentment best when he said, "He who has so little knowledge of human nature as to seek happiness by changing anything, but his own disposition will waste his life in fruitless efforts and multiply grief which he purposes to remove." In other words, your attitude can change every aspect of your life. Why then do so many of us fall for external happiness by seeking and acquiring materialistic items rather than internal fulfillment? The feelings of satisfaction that come from great achievements are only momentary flashes in your life. Like a candle flame, at some point, the fame and fortune become just a flicker in your life that will surely dim with time. If happiness is a choice we make with regard to our attitude, IT CANNOT BE BOUGHT OR WON. It's that simple. I don't see how anyone can live a life of happiness with a piss-poor attitude. Personally, that would not work for me.

Your attitude evolves from the choices you make, which means only you can control your attitude. Attitude, whether positive or negative, holds the greatest power in an individual's character. It is the only characteristic that can truly make a difference in your life and in the lives of the people around you. The amount of impact your attitude can have on yourself and others is the choice only you can make. The key ingredient behind this interaction is the determination behind your ability to make the choice. The issue with attitude is that many people believe their attitudes are a fixed attribute that cannot be changed. By acquiring the knowledge that your attitude is a choice, you can choose the correct attitude that will ultimately lead to positive outcomes. The first step in deciding to have a positive attitude is embedded in the decision of you taking responsibility for your attitude. Only you are responsible for your attitude, no one else. It's up to you to decide whether it is positive or piss-poor.

Over the years, I have asked myself many times, "Does your family make you happy? Does your wife bring you happiness? Do your children bring you joy? Does your job make you accomplished?" My response every time is, "NO!" Nobody can make another person truly happy. It is my duty, my responsibility, my decision to make myself happy by deciding my own attitude. Unfortunately, many of us never learn this concept, which leads many to choose an unhappy life of depression and despair. I believe in my own simple formula for generating happiness; if you want today to be an awesome day, take charge of the way you view your day and the world you live in. Is the cup half empty, half full, or always full? True, there are events and people in our lives we cannot change; however, we do have the power to change our outlook through a positive attitude. I believe the cup is always full, never empty. Your glass remains full of something— whether it is gas or a liquid, it is up to you to visualize it that way.

Another practice I use to generate a positive attitude is to think, act, speak, and conduct myself like the person I want to be. If you want to change your attitude, then change your mind and thought patterns. View the world from outside the box and take different approaches to whatever a given scenario might be. Start by believing you can improve on who you are and think of the ways you can change into the person you want to become. "I hate my life. I wish I could be the person I am supposed to be," says the person with the piss-poor attitude, living day to day with a glass that is empty mentality. Without change, a pessimistic attitude will lead you down a path of despair.

Many years ago, my grandfather taught me a lesson that still holds true today. The lesson is this: "Sonny boy, it's important to find something positive in everything you do. It will not always be easy to find something positive in everything, but if you try hard enough, you will find good in everything, even in the worst of situations." For many years, I searched for the meaning of this lesson as I became more and more invested in material things. Our nature leads us to dwell on the negatives rather than the positives. In some of my worst situations, it was difficult to find the light in the darkest places. Now, I look at every situation as an opportunity to find goodness in the world. Do you think I'm crazy for this? You're entitled to your opinion, but this is a philosophy that has become a cornerstone in how I live. I choose to consider the fact that I am still here as a good outcome and enough reason to not let my attitude be affected negatively.

A friend shared the following with me:

> Dear Lord,
>   So far today, I am doing all right. I have not gossiped, lost my temper, been greedy, grumpy,

nasty, selfish, or self-indulgent. I have not whined, cursed, or eaten any chocolate.

However, I am going to get out of bed in a few minutes, and I will need a lot more help after that. AMEN!

Ask yourself and be honest, where do you stand with your attitude? Are you choosing daily to have a positive influential attitude? What do you do when you let your piss-poor attitude take control of you? I believe my attitude is more important than facts themselves, more important than any skills I have, more important than the education I have completed, more important than my past, more important than the money I have, more important than any circumstance I have experienced, more important than any failures or successes I have ever achieved, more than what you think, more than what others think or what others say or do. To me, my attitude stands at the top of my character hierarchy pyramid. What I have found is that life is less about what happens to me and more about how I react to it. It is my choice to use my attitude to make every day of my life an outstanding day. Attitude is everything.

Living Well

What does a better life and living well mean to you? Before you can begin your journey down a path to a better life and living well, you should have some idea of what that means to you. It is important to know that *success* and *"living well"* have different definitions to all of us. To some, living well means traveling the world and investing time visiting other cultures. To others, it means having the time and money to live the luxurious lifestyle they always wanted. Some of us believe it is having more time to devote to our favorite pursuits, more time to spend with the people we love or working in our purpose.

When you envision success, what does it look like? When you ask yourself what it means to "live well," what do you imagine? Some of us have been raised to believe that success requires arduous amounts of work and dedication toward a specific profession. When you consider the idea of living well, your thoughts may conflict with that belief. To you, living well might not entail strenuous work and dedication toward a profession. It might mean having an abundance of leisure time. The statement, "It's five o'clock somewhere" may hold a higher value for you.

To fully embrace what you envision success to be, it is important for you to first examine your long-held beliefs. Do you believe that living well means possessing luxury items like a new car and a large home, or do you believe that living well means being able to spend more time at home and less time at work? How do your beliefs support your vision? How are your beliefs keeping you from the successful life you want? As you consider your beliefs, ask yourself why you believe something to be true. You may discover that you have held on to a belief only because you never thought to question it.

Creating time to develop a vision of success for your future is a necessity. Close your eyes and begin by imagining an ideal day where you spend your time pursuing your passions and living a simplistic lifestyle. Once you have this vision fixed in your mind, write it down. As you describe this vision on paper, it will begin to form and take shape. You will begin to imagine your future in a unique way as you see it take life. As you write down your vision of your future, you will find that there is excess baggage that is weighing you down. This excess baggage requires you to take immediate action. It must be eliminated from your life. The actual steps you need to take will become clearer and more precise as your vision of success takes shape.

When you consider your vision of success, does it include acquiring materialistic items and performing time-consuming tasks? Before you add more to your life, you need to perform a self-inventory of what you already possess. Look at your personal belongings as well as your personal attributes. Chances are, you already possess all the skills and knowledge you will ever need. The question is, "Why are you letting these attributes waste away as you watch others pass you by?" Most of us already have the needed enthusiasm but lack the courage to take the risk. A life well lived often starts by appreciating what attributes you already have and mustering the courage to act on the ones you lack.

Simple living is an easy concept to grasp but confuses many of us when putting it into action. To live a simple lifestyle, begin by embracing what you have, accumulate less, and shift your time, energy, and money toward what is truly important. If you have no idea what is truly important to you, then simple living will appear to be a quantum physics equation that you have no idea how to solve. Ask yourself, what do I want? What do you truly want in this life? Knowing yourself and staying true to the person looking back at you in the mirror will help you embrace the world around you as you learn to live well with what you have. When you think you know the answer to the previous two questions, ask yourself why. Continue to ask why until you establish that you have indeed found the root of the question. Remember, as you continue to ask questions, you only receive the answers to the questions you ask. If you are unwilling to ask yourself why, you will never receive what you are truly seeking in this life. If you are willing to search and endure the journey, the universe will deliver.

Have you ever watched the TV show *Hoarders*? If not, this reality TV show reveals the life of people who live a life of extreme consumption and are unwilling to part ways with any given item in their home. As consumers, we accumulate items throughout our life without putting much thought into why. I know people who purchased clothes five years ago and still have the tags on them. These same people will go to the store, buy a trinket because of the awesome sale price. Once purchased, they go home, put it on the shelf or in the closet just to turn around months or years later and find themselves buying some of the same items they already have. When you know who you are, live a simple life and stay true to yourself, the need to acquire unnecessary merchandise becomes less important. Instead of allowing the impulse of acquiring to take over your inner self, you're able to stop and ask yourself if this purchase supports you, your needs, and your goals. When you silence your impulse of mass consumption, you are able to transition to a conscious consumption lifestyle.

Living well with what you have means you have become grateful for the people and items you have surrounded yourself with. Living well also means that you love yourself. This type of love is not a narcissistic staring contest with your reflection in a swimming hole. This type of love is one where you are content, confident, and hold a strong respect for who you are. To find this place where you love yourself and can surround yourself with people who love and support you, you must first find your inner being. You must find that place deep inside where you are confident with who you are, respect where you have come from, and are content with knowing you can take on whatever life has to throw at you. You must know your strengths and sharpen your weaknesses so they may turn into strengths. Staying true to who you are and remaining honest with the people around you will enable you to create a life of well-being. Instead of always wanting and needing more, try being grateful for what you have. This gratitude plays a significant role in developing the mind-set of personal awareness that is essential for moving forward, away from old habits, and toward a new life of well-being.

Staying true to yourself also requires a great deal of awareness. You must be able to listen to your instincts and follow your thoughts while sorting out temporary emotions and impulses that construct the vision you have of your life. Living well is about developing a lifestyle that supports who you are. It is impossible to develop and maintain this lifestyle if you are unwilling to stay true to who you are. Every day, distractions will bombard you with messages that are contrary to your vision of your future life. These distractions have great potential to lead you astray from your path. Society will lead you to believe that all the latest gadgets and new fashion lines are must-haves in order to be accepted by others. This lifestyle can and will wear you down if you do not know who you are and what you want from your life.

For a growing number of people, the definition of "living well" is changing. Instead of filling their life with material goods and splurging on luxury items, they have decided to live a simpler life that they enjoy and love. It is about living life on their own terms, free from the shackles of having to fit into a predetermined category, career, or lifestyle. Living well means designing a future for yourself that is rewarding, satisfying, and focused on supporting who you are and what you want from life. For some, the realization of how shitty their life is and the overwhelming lack of fulfillment becomes clear. With an epiphany, it becomes abundantly clear they live to acquire shit and have successfully surrounded themselves with huge amounts of shit and in turn realize they have this shitty lifestyle they cannot seem to change. In the end, the homeless man on the corner may be happier when you consider he may be living the life he desires. The life that makes him happy.

A shift is necessary. It begins by living well with what you already have. This shift will require simplifying what you already have and making the necessary lifestyle changes. Ultimately, it is about being happier with what you have and creating a life that supports what you really want.

FOUR AREAS IN THE PURSUIT OF LIVING WELL THAT WILL HELP YOU:

- Ask questions
- Spring cleaning
- Set goals and break free from old habits
- Moving forward

Ask Questions

"Learn from yesterday, live for today, hope for tomorrow. The important thing is not to stop questioning," a quote from Albert Einstein that holds many truths. Asking questions is the first step to knowing what you want, who you are, and in determining who you want to be. When reflecting on your life and how it applies to this quote, ask yourself the questions that are listed below. As you continue to read, grab a pen and paper/journal and write down these questions along with your brutally honest answers. You may surprise yourself with what you come up with.

What do you enjoy about your life?

Think about your life. Consider where you are now and consider where you want to be. Are you doing exactly what you intended for your life? Or are you day dreaming your days away wishing you were somewhere else? Write down your hobbies, where you work, and how you spend your time. Write down the names of the people in your life and identify the items in your home that you have an emotional connection with. Reflect on the memories that bring you happiness then note the specific individuals you share them with. Write down what you love about your life and how it brings you a sense of fulfillment. If you had to prioritize three aspects of your life, what would they be and how do they support your pursuit of living well?

Answering the tough questions allows you to begin to see what is important to you, how things are important to you, and why things are important to you. You may discover that some of the things that you love most are the things that you spend very little time on. You may love to travel but find that travel is at the bottom of your current priority list. Take your time answering this question. Establishing a strong foundation is important for moving forward.

What can you live without?

Consider your life. Where have you been, where are you now, and where do you want to be? While considering your life in these three questions, try to identify the things that you can live without. Write them down. When I mention the word *things*, I am not just referring to belongings, possessions, and assets but everything that is a part of your life including places, people, and relationships. You may find that the things you identify are possessions, belongings, and people you really don't care for.

Answering this question will highlight the important aspects of your life that are creating roadblocks to your success. You waste time and expend energy detouring through life while forgetting the important people and things you really care about. Break free of the dead weight that is holding you back while considering the items and people that are really important.

Do you spend your time wisely?

How do you spend your time? Write down the activities and people that you spend most of your time with. Divide the paper in two to create two columns. Label one column "time yielding success," the other labeled "wasteful time." Spend one week to a month tracking your time throughout each day. For each activity, write down the amount of time in minutes you spend. You may be surprised at what you discover, and the results may be eye-opening.

Performing this activity will help you recognize how you can make changes in your day-to-day life by dropping the dead weight and optimizing the time that provides you the most success. You will be able to identify activities to optimize and take advantage of what makes you happy and fulfilled rather than spending time on the excess baggage holding you back. For example, you may find that you waste eight hours a week cleaning your home, scrubbing the tub and the baseboards week in and week out, when you would much rather spend this time writing your book or starting your own business. Knowing where your time is spent is vital to bring change in your life. When you become efficient with your time and understand where your time is being wasted, you are rewarded with more time in a day than you previously thought.

What are your strengths and weaknesses?

This is a question asked many times by many people, but few will consider. It's difficult to write down personal strengths. Our society and human consciousness tend to dwell on our weaknesses and failures rather than our strengths and successes. Write down five personal strengths and five personal weaknesses. Also, for each you identify, write your reasoning. This information will help you identify what positive changes you need to make in your life. You might find that one of your weaknesses is the lack of organization. By knowing this, you can act to find solutions that will turn your weakness of disorganization into a strength of organization.

What is your perfect day?

If you were to paint a perfect day on a canvas, what would it look like? Would it resemble an impressionistic Monet painting depicting the idea of living in the moment, or a surrealistic Picasso masterpiece where a dream becomes a form of hyperreality? Close your eyes for a moment and imagine your perfect day. I'm not talking about a day sipping wine while being fed grapes on the French Riviera. Sure, that seems like a perfect day, but is this the type of day that best fits your everyday lifestyle? I'm talking about a normal perfect day for you. Write down what you imagined to be your perfect day.

Example: A normal perfect day for someone who wants to write a book might start with an hour of writing, a day at a job they love, and then time in the evening with loved ones relaxing, talking, and laughing.

What steps are you taking that will launch you toward what you really want in your life?

What actions are you currently doing that helps you move your life toward your description of a perfect day? That perfect day you imagined in the last question. This can be anything from material objects to your relationships with the people around you. Write your answer down.

The person who wants to write more and clean less might be helped by a partner who is happy to clean a little more, or a vacant space in the house might be easily converted to a writing office.

What is holding you back from moving toward what you really want in your life?

Take a moment to consider your surroundings from a different perspective. Write down the things that are getting in your way and holding you underwater as you drown in a lifestyle that makes you truly unhappy.

A large house that has a tremendous amount of upkeep may be something that does not help you if you want to be a writer. A giant car payment does not help you if you are working in a job that you want to cut back on the amount of overtime you must work to sustain your lifestyle. A fifty-dollar-a-week Starbucks habit does not help if you are struggling to pay off debts to obtain financial freedom.

Are you getting the idea? I hope so! What is preventing you from living your perfect day?

You may find several of these questions are difficult to answer, and it may take you a few days, even a few weeks, to answer them all as completely and honestly as possible. Once you have answered the questions, you have what you need to begin making your necessary life changes.

Spring Cleaning

Every spring, millions of households across the country begin to declutter from the hoarding habits of winter. As the weather changes from winter to spring, the transition humans make from being a hibernating bear to a wandering wolf pack begins. Just as we take time to spring clean our homes year after year, we should also perform a little spring cleaning of our personal lives. Making room by decluttering your life is essential. You may have a house full of stuff or a social life filled with drama that requires spring cleaning. If you take a hard look at all the junk you have been hoarding and carrying around with you, you may realize that most of that junk does not serve you. If you take an honest look at all your belongings and excess baggage that you continue to hold on to, it should become obvious to you that some, if not most of it, does not make you happy. Holding on to material things and dead relationships do not solve any problems; rather, they create problems for you. Clutter is stressful and holds you back from moving toward what you really want in your life.

For some, renting a dumpster and purging their hoarding lifestyle is very tempting. If ridding yourself of the excess baggage you carry is really what you want to do, then get started. But for others, taking the approach of systematically going through their belongings, room by room, over time is more ideal. As you go through your things, try to consider whether each item helps you or whether it is time to throw the junk away. Start slowly so you do not become overwhelmed. It is possible that if you purge your home in a weekend, you may throw something away that you may later regret. This will not only waste your time as you search for the lost item but also money as you may need to replace it. As you move through your home, room by room, you can become overwhelmed regardless if you start slowly. But if you are feeling ambitious, try beginning in the most cluttered room. This might be your kitchen or your walk-in closet. The important thing to remember during this decluttering event is that you started.

To make this process less painful, organization experts recommend making four piles: the Keep, the Donate, the Toss, and the Sell. The items you keep are the items that you love most, cannot be replaced, and help you to live your perfect life. These items are things that you know you will continue to use and love years from now. Next, donate items that are in good condition but no longer serve a purpose for you. Throw away the broken items and the things you know people will not want. Lastly, sell the items that you can gain money from. Having a yard sale or listing the items on an auction website is a great way to make extra cash from the items you no longer want.

Another approach to decluttering is to donate, sell, or toss ten items each week. Or you can work on getting rid of one thing every day. Whichever way you choose to go about your decluttering does not matter. The idea is to begin and stay consistent. The way you go about separating what you keep, donate, toss, or sell depends largely on your current clutter and your needs.

Now that you have decluttered your home and life, it is important to have an organized space for what remains. This means making sure your closets, pantry, and other storage areas are also organized. There is a reason for stores called "the Container Store." Utilize them!

It doesn't take a genius to realize that decluttering and staying organized is important. By now, you must be thinking why make such a big deal about this topic. Essentially, when you declutter your life, it provides you with a clean slate. It allows you to get rid of the items that are holding you back from living your best life. Decluttering forces you to truly prioritize the things that you want and need.

Setting Goals and Breaking Free from Old Habits

After you have decluttered your home and your life, it is time to look at setting goals that will help you live a better life with what you already have. The next step is to begin making positive changes to your lifestyle. Once these positive changes become routine, turn your focus to getting rid of the habits that are holding you back and add new habits that keep you moving forward.

One of the habits that will help you avoid focusing on spending your money and acquiring new unnecessary items is the habit of gratitude. Be grateful! You can embrace gratitude in many ways, and you can start each day by thinking about all the things you are grateful for then write them in a journal. You can also begin saying *please* and *thank you* at specific times during the day. Yes, this sounds crazy and unordinary, but it works for me, and it will work for you.

How often do you find yourself shopping online? Do you fill up your Amazon cart buying items on a whim because it makes you feel good? For many people, shopping is a habit that leads to short-term satisfaction and yields a home full of unwanted stuff. This is not only financially wasteful but inhibits you from moving toward the life you really want. Do you even know what your spending habits are? If not, there are several ways to find out. The best way to help yourself is to simply stop shopping for the sake of shopping. This is tough to do. It's like telling a smoker to quit smoking. That temporary satisfaction you experience will soon fade, and the need for purchasing will return. It is almost like a drug; the temporary sense of euphoria is so powerful that people have become bankrupt as they max out multiple credit cards. When looking for happiness in shopping, most times you only create a place of loneliness. Finding happiness in hobbies or other activities that replace your need to shop is key. Instead of shopping on the weekends or surfing the Internet looking for that next awesome deal with free shipping, try other activities such as building furniture, hiking, fishing, mountain biking, painting, knitting, cooking, or joining a softball league; whatever it is, find something that you can channel your energy into that is positive and productive other than shopping.

Like most people, if you break something, you replace it…right? Not anymore. Instead of replacing items that need a little TLC, try being creative and use some of your skills to create something new. If you do not have any skills, maybe it is time to learn some. Doing it yourself is a great way to add personality to your home, to provide you with a sense of satisfaction, and to keep items that you love in your possession. If you are not handy, then maybe it is time to spend some energy learning craftsmanship. If you find that you are really not the handyman type, consider searching the millions of DIY videos on YouTube that show you how to fix any issue you can imagine. You will develop a sense of accomplishment when you are finished.

Find and focus on your passions. Find activities and pursuits that make you feel happy deep within. Whether you enjoy creating home brew beer to making homemade wine or writing travel books or building websites, find the activity that you are passionate about. Living well with what you have is not just focused on clearing out material items; it is also about clearing away the pursuits and tasks that do not bring you joy or a sense of self-worth. Sure, no day is without some menial tasks, but if the bulk of your life is spent on pursuits that make you smile, then you are living well.

Moving Forward

By now, you should be getting a good picture in your head as to what a simpler life looks like. The vision should be a life that is full of love and meaning that has been defined by you as a good life. It is imperative for you to create change and commit to your own path and purpose. If you want to live well with what you have, then you must make a commitment to yourself that the path you are on is the path you are going to take. No path is the same; everyone walks down a different path. In its simplest form, it comes down to not adding more clutter and distractions to your life while making the major changes that are necessary for your life's journey. The path you take might require you to downsize your home, sell your home, or move to another city or state. It can also mean a new job, career, or becoming a business owner.

If you start by committing to the change your life needs, what is the next step? It is to start setting small goals to help you transition to the life that will give you what you desire. Small goals can be anything. These goals can be simply cleaning out your closet and only keeping the clothes that you wear and love. It might mean taking a class that will help you start a new career or business. Start setting small goals with a larger goal in mind. Create a plan to follow through and commit yourself to making it happen. Then pull the trigger. Give it all you have to make it come true.

Start living your life as if you are already where you want to be. You have envisioned your ideal day, so you know what it looks like. You have made a list of the things and people that support you as well as lists about your strengths, weaknesses, and the things that hold you back. You have an idea about how you want to live your life. So, act now! By now, you should know what you want in this life. Start living as if you have already achieved your goals and love every day you have. This is important because it creates a shift in your mind-set. Instead of saying that you are trying to live well with what you have, say that you are living well with what you have. Instead of saying that you want to write a book, say that you are writing a book. See the difference?

Approaching your life as if you have already achieved your goals empowers you to take steps each day to make it true. When you cut down to the "essentials" and what is most important to you in your life, you may be surprised at what it takes to make you truly happy.

Controlling Your Anger

Whatever is begun in anger ends in shame.
—Benjamin Franklin

External Stimuli that Generates Anger

It is all too common to blame work, stress, having to pay the bills as the external stimulus causing anger in our lives. The truth is, there is nothing external that is triggering your anger; it is brought on by internal processes. If work or bills provoked anger in everyone, the workplace would be one pissed-off warzone needing one big chill pill. But if we look within, we realize that we have choices when it comes to being angry. When you look within, you realize that external stimulus is not the cause of your anger. It is you. You generate the anger within. Many people are working and paying their bills without being wrapped up in anger. It is important to learn how to identify what triggers an angry feeling within you, which in turn will help you identify the steps needed to channel this energy in to a positive reaction.

Know Your Triggers

Our anger can be triggered by anything—from someone stealing your parking spot to an overdraft fee from your bank. Here are a few anger triggers you might recognize:

People

- Boss
- Mother-in-law
- Romantic partner
- One of your children

Places

- The office
- At home
- The supermarket
- A parking lot

Things

- Your car
- Your computer
- Your broken water pipe
- Your broken home appliance

Events

- Holidays with the family
- Business meetings
- Phone calls with difficult people
- Paying your bills every month

Once you understand what triggers your anger, you can develop strategies to curb your anger before it causes you to fly off the handle.

Understanding the Source of Your Anger

If you hate paying bills, you are probably experiencing stress for many obvious, and perhaps less obvious reasons. The obvious one is that you are offtrack with your budget and are struggling to make ends meet as you live paycheck to paycheck. Every bill you receive is a stressful experience that makes you feel trapped and helpless. If you procrastinate paying your bills, you might get a short-term feeling of relief from the responsibility of paying what is owed each month. But this can backfire in several ways, leaving you in a worse position than if you had just paid the bills. Everyone knows, or should know, that paying bills late can lead to fines, fees, and surcharges, leading to more money spent and less money in your bank account. This leads to an even more difficult financial situation in the long term, which can become an anger trigger.

Emotions Other than Anger

There are other emotional masks we all wear that is involved in paying the bills that might be less obvious but no less powerful triggers. You might be infuriated by the fact that you are working so hard at a job that you dread going to, yet you still cannot make ends meet. If you have been careless with money in the past, you might be angry at yourself in the present.

If you feel your family is irresponsible with money, this will cause resentment and turmoil between family members. Some individuals feel a sense of guilt as they cannot provide more for the ones they love. This perception of guilt can and will lead to a sense of failure every time you sit down to pay the bills. This underlying feeling or negative mental chatter will trigger your anger rather than the actual act of paying the bill. If you believe the sources of your anger are external to yourself, remember that nothing and no one "makes you feel" anger or any other emotion. Anger will surface just like other emotions, and it is up to you to choose how you handle it. You can allow anger to get the best of you or brush it aside, pay the bills, and move on with yourself.

How Guilt and Resentment Can Fuel Your Anger

A man that studieth revenge keeps his own wounds green.
—Francis Bacon

Have you ever had a situation that caused you to be concerned about having anger issues? Think about that situation and then trace the triggers that set you off during that event. One of the most common mistakes we make when assessing our anger issues is to blame external things as making us angry. Have you ever considered that the very anger you experience is actually caused by inner turmoil deep within? Being quick to anger is usually a sign that something in your life is out of balance. It is an indicator that something needs to be worked on to create or regain a sense of balance in your life. Anger is often an indication that other emotions are at play, such as guilt and resentment.

Guilt. Guilt is the result of having a sense you have done something wrong or of having fallen short of someone else's expectations. It could be something minor such as showing up late for a date or forgetting to buy a birthday gift. These situations also lead to resentment resulting from someone expecting something from you or feeling that you have let them down. Parents can often make children feel guilty when their expectations are not met—spoken, unspoken or implied. This can trigger resentment as well, especially if you feel as though you are jumping through hoops to satisfy the other person. It can feel as though whatever you do just never seems to be good enough.

Resentment. No one likes to feel as if they are a failure. The more pressure you place on yourself, the more stress you will feel. Most of us rarely perform our best when we are constantly under stress, overworked, and not getting enough sleep. You might start to feel guilty that you are working so hard that you are neglecting your family, which can lead to you feeling trapped and resentful. You have expended all your resources to make ends meet, yet it never seems to get any better.

Sometimes, people feel a sense of resentment toward their partner or even their kids as they feel their efforts are being taken for granted. They feel as if their family or partner is taking their hard work and putting it to the side and putting their own needs first. Another example is the person who works long hard hours all week and wants to have a little time to themselves over the weekend, only to be presented with a mile-long honey-do list. If the list isn't completed in a timely manner, they are reminded of the individual items on this list repeatedly until the nagging becomes unbearable. This "nagging" can lead to resentment. This in turn can lead to heated arguments that get blown way out of proportion, all resulting from an irrelevant misunderstanding of the original underlying issue.

Secrets and lies. One of the most common reasons for divorce has been cited as financial issues. Many people equate their worth as human beings with the career they have or how much money they earn in their profession. When financial problems arise, these types of people hide behind their egos and are scared to admit their poor financial decisions. They do not like to admit to their partner that they might have blown $1,000 at the casino or might not be earning as much as what they told their partner. Some people will even keep their disastrous financial past a secret from their partner, locked away in a filing cabinet. This same type of couple will eagerly apply for a mortgage loan to buy their dream home, only to get rejected due to having murky financial pasts that neither one knew about, which leads to a disastrous ending.

The blame game never works, and nobody wins; it just fuels more anger and resentment. One of the best ways to manage this anger and resentment is to cut the roots that allow it to grow. This means living more authentically and honestly, connecting with your feelings both positive and negative, without trying to run from them or suppress them. Once you start to do this, you will notice a difference in your level of anger and quality of life.

Different Ways to Express Anger

Anger is just one letter short of danger.
—Eleanor Roosevelt

Anger is an emotion we are born with, and it is inevitable that we will experience this feeling at some point in our life. Anger is natural, and to not express it in a controlled way is unhealthy. The problem we face is the misconception that anger is wrong and we must hold it deep within. Anger is not the issue; it is the way we express anger that is the problem. If you feel that your level of anger has elevated, and it is starting to affect your closest relationships negatively, it is time to consider anger management strategies that can help you express your anger in more productive ways.

Taking Time

The first technique in managing your anger is simple, and many of us may have tried it before. It is the age-old technique of counting to ten, forcing yourself to pause for a length of time before doing or saying anything you will regret later. Once this brief period has passed, then you can explain and express your emotions while explaining why you feel angry.

Another technique is stepping away from the situation. A self-proclaimed "time-out." You can say, "I am sorry, I feel angry, so I need a few minutes before I can deal with this." Then remove yourself from the situation so you can be alone until you feel you gathered your thoughts.

Shake It Off

Another technique to work off your underlying anger is through exercise or sports. Some busy executives enjoy using sports such as basketball or racquetball to rid their aggression. A simple walk around the block to breathe some fresh air will work wonders. Yoga and Tai Chi will center and ground you, helping reduce stress so you are much less prone to fly off the handle.

Taking a break at lunch and small ones throughout the day may seem counterproductive, but you can get more done as you lower your stress and increase your concentration levels.

Own Your Feelings

Own your anger! This is a strategy many of us refuse to use as we let our egos lead the way. No one is "making you feel" angry. It is a natural emotion we all experience, and it is your choice to allow anger to take control of you and your actions. Only you can prevent yourself from making the wrong choice. I have found through trial and error that the strategy that works best for me is to ignore and not waste time on the things that cause me to become angry. An African proverb that helps me stay the course goes like this: "The lion doesn't turn around when the small dog barks." Be the lion.

Expressing Anger Effectively

Anger management also means learning how to express yourself in a healthy way. Many of us try to avoid conflict. The truth is, we are not avoiding anything. Our feelings still build deep within us like a pressure cooker until we explode, destroying the relationships around us.

The following are a couple of ways to express your anger effectively without harming the people around you. Start by learning to say, "I feel angry now because…" rather than, "I am angry because…" When you say, "I feel angry now because…," you distance yourself from the emotion, which helps you to realize it is only temporary allowing new feelings to surface sooner rather than later. The second way is to express yourself with *I* phrases only, not *you*. When you say, "You made me feel angry," you are not taking responsibility for or control of your feelings. A third approach is to avoid using absolutes such as, "You ALWAYS" and "You NEVER."

Manage Expectations

Another key to controlling your anger is to manage expectations and understanding. Your anger may be the result of you expecting one thing to happen and instead another does. Or you thought you and your boss or spouse had agreed to X and they have done Y or expect Y. Remembering that there are two sides to every story will help you maintain control of your anger instead of it controlling you. Anger management is not about never feeling angry; rather, it is about learning how to express your anger in a positive manner that will not damage or destroy relationships.

Anger Management

One of the quickest ways to lose respect is to have an anger issue. For a period in my life, I was a very angry person. I had no idea why until I received professional help. My anger was based in survivor's guilt. I was angry at the world for the death of my friends when they were killed in a terrorist ambush. I felt, in many ways, that it was my fault they died. I should have been in their place. We traded shifts, and if we had not done so, I would have been on the bus instead of my friends. I was angry and spent many nights staring at the ceiling as I lay awake. I could not sleep, I was unable to control my drinking, I felt my life slipping away from me, and there was nothing I could do to stop it. I was angry because during that time, I truly believed life was unfair and not worth living. I felt life was so unfair, I lowered myself to acting like a toddler having temper tantrums. Yes, it was worse. I broke things, threw things, hit things, and had no tolerance for people. There were times when I was out-of-control angry that I made some of the greatest speeches I have ever regretted making.

Anger made me feel powerful and in control, when the opposite was true. Anger damages relationships with friends, family, and colleagues. I have said and done things I later regretted and was unable to correct as the damage from my behavior was already done. Do you have an anger problem? If you are worried that your anger controls you rather than you are controlling your anger, then it is time to use the anger management strategies listed above. Mastering anger management is not easy; it takes time, effort, and commitment. If you do have anger management issues and do nothing about it, you lose every time. In fact, you can lose everything right up to including your life.

What I found to be the starting point in controlling my anger was admitting I had an anger-control problem. One of the biggest problems people have with anger is recognizing it in the first place.

We all show anger in different ways. For some of us, it is obvious; for others, not so much. You do not have to scream, shout, or throw things to have an anger problem. Once you admit you have an anger problem, you have a starting point to work on your anger control and lead a happier life. Yes, angry people are unhappy people. And for some, like myself, my unhappiness had a lot to do with my anger; and my anger fed my unhappiness. It is a hard cycle to break free from.

We all have words for anger as we try to define this emotion— *stress*, *disappointment*, *frustration*, *irritation*, *annoyance*, and many others. What these words really add up to is your expectation of what you WANT your life to be like and what your life IS like. The greater the disconnect, the greater the anger.

Your anger can also be magnified by a perception that someone is "DOING SOMETHING TO YOU," either accidentally or on purpose. This sense of being wronged can lead you to your breaking point, pushing your anger way out of proportion. You do not have to look any farther than the nightly news to understand how this works. An individual is arrested for breaking the law, but an entire community becomes angered not at the bad guy but at the police. The community believes they were wronged and run to the streets as they destroy their own neighborhoods. Maybe the police were not there in the first place to stop the crime. Maybe the community does not want the police in their community. Maybe the community believes they were wronged, which results in an angry response that is way out of proportion.

Some people process their anger without thought and react by "flying off the handle" over the littlest thing. Do you have a boss or coworker that is like this, or perhaps maybe you even do this? People who fly off the handle in an outburst of anger over the littlest thing lack self-control and are clearly candidates for anger management counseling. Constantly making a mountain out of a molehill is unhealthy and can result in damaged relationships that cannot be fixed. Some individuals dwell on their anger, letting it fester within their mind. Like a volcano waiting to explode, these individuals are holding their anger in until the pressure is too much. When they finally lash out, they can do more damage than someone who merely throws a fit regularly to blow off steam. The individuals who hold every bit of anger in are the ones who hurt people, break things, and often hurt themselves when they finally blow up in anger. This happens because people rarely choose the precise moment to let their anger out. As scientists are unable to predict when a volcano will erupt, people are unable to do the same with their peers who hold their anger in. One minute, they are fine; then someone pushes their button just right, and BOOM! If you are tired of dealing with the consequences of your anger, anger management is a key area for you to seek out and master.

Once you admit that you have anger control issues, the next step is learning how to deal with and manage it daily. Learning anger management allows you to control the anger you experience in a healthy way rather than a destructive way. We can all benefit from learning how to manage our own anger in a healthy way. Things that happen to you are no one else's fault but your own, and only you can make yourself happy, only you can make yourself sad, only you can make yourself angry, and only you can learn how to change your situation for the better. As with everything else, managing your anger control issues does not include placing the blame on others. It also does not mean trying to suppress your anger to the point where you become physically and emotionally ill. Anger management is simply learning how to express anger in a positive way that will be honest and productive.

What needs to be learned first about anger management is that while it is a natural emotion that affects all of us, you have a choice about what you do with the anger you feel. Think about it: do you really have to act out the moment you feel angry? Some of us do. Or are you able to take a step back, process the feeling, and channel it in a positive way? The correct approach is to take a moment to determine what is angering you, why it is angering you, and whether anything constructive can be done about the issue to help relieve your anger.

As a public speaker, I have met many people who have approached me and asked, "Well, Jeff, what if nothing can be done?" I always respond with, "Should you dwell on the issue or just let it pass by like a cloud in the sky? Why do you need to dwell on what made you angry in the first place? Is it doing anything to help fix the issue?" After these answers, I usually receive a response that goes something like "WELL, THAT'S JUST IMPOSSIBLE TO DO WHEN YOU ARE ANGRY!" The fact is, it can be done. We all experience a wide range of feelings throughout the day; we feel hungry, thirsty, hot, cold. And we have ways of dealing with each stimulus by eating, drinking, turning on the AC or the heat. We do not get angry with our body betraying us. We do not dwell for hours on being hungry, thirsty, or feeling upset every time we think about it. We do not hold a grudge for years because we were hungry or thirsty once during the week. Being hungry or thirsty is just one of the many feelings that come and go throughout the day and is managed accordingly.

Whether you accept the premise or not, by now, you should understand that being angry is a choice. To focus on your anger is your choice. It's your choice to either do something about it or let it go. If you find yourself gritting your teeth over something that happened ages ago at work or years ago with a parent or a loved one, you are still allowing that feeling to control you rather than freeing yourself by letting it go. There is nothing you can do about events you have endured in your past except to learn from them and realize that moving on is liberating. WHATEVER HAPPENED IN YOUR PAST HAPPENED IN YOUR PAST. IT IS YOUR CHOICE TO ALLOW IT TO KEEP AFFECTING YOUR LIFE OR TO GET OVER IT. By utilizing anger management skills, you can process both past and present anger. This will require you to be honest with yourself by admitting you have an anger control issue in the first place.

Anger management is no different from dealing with your attitude, gaining respect through being assertive or knowing if something is right for you or not. Anger management is taking ownership of your own feelings. No one is doing anything to you. People are not "making you feel" anything. The feeling is within you, and since it is within you, you can take control of it. Once you understand the reason you are feeling angry, you are on the right path toward dealing with anger in a healthy, productive way.

Anger management teaches the techniques that are necessary to manage anger emotions before they ever start. Effective anger management techniques can help decrease the frequency of your anger or, if you do become angry, help reduce the duration of staying angry. If you want to live a happier healthier life, it is time to tame your temper.

Learning what anger management techniques work best for you is a process of personal learning and self-assessment. The "one-size-fits-all" approach does not apply here. For some, keeping an anger management journal helps them keep track of what works and what does not, what made them angry, and what they did to free themselves from the crippling grip of anger. Doing a self-assessment and reflecting on what you find out about yourself can be a painful process as feelings you have suppressed for years begin to show their ugly face. This time, however, will be different; you will be ready to suppress the issues from your past that make you boil deep inside. If this happens, take note of what the issue is, do not let it take control of you, and do not let it paralyze you. This will be difficult, but remember, you are in control of your life and emotions. Once you feel the sense of empowerment, your life changes. It will be much easier to manage your emotions, including anger.

It is important to understand that your unruly anger is not a condition, it is a process and emotion. It is a symptom of your life being out of balance. It is your personal alarm system letting you know that you need to make some adjustments in your life. These adjustments will fix burning the candle at both ends—not getting enough rest, skipping meals, spending most of your time working, not exercising or not allowing time for yourself. If you fail to make the needed adjustments, it will result in small irritations appearing larger than they are, creating an unnecessary outburst of anger that you will surely regret. You cannot run on an empty tank and expect to perform at your best. Make the adjustments you need to make.

Anger often masks other emotions you are feeling. Stress, depression, anxiety, substance abuse—including caffeine, tobacco, alcohol, drugs, impulse habits (uncontrollable spending, eating, gambling, sex, drinking)—fear of abandonment, fear of commitment, lack of self-esteem, or poor coping are just a few examples of emotions that people experience but are often masked by anger. Poor coping skills also enables you to easily believe the myth that there is nothing you can do to control your anger when in fact, you indeed have choices.

Like a broken record, people often tell me repeatedly that they do not have a choice when it comes to controlling and expressing their anger when in fact, they do. You have a choice when you shout at someone or throw things. Anger management helps you create smarter choices in relation to how you deal with your emotions. We often become angry and irritable when someone at work keeps inter-rupting while you are trying to get your work done. But this sense of irritation and anger is a choice. You have the choice on how you deal with it. You can ignore it, you can count to ten and then deal with it, you can communicate your feelings in a respectful way by requesting they come back when you have finished, you can let them know you will visit them when you have finished what you are working on, or you can change the situation so it is less stressful by dealing with it then and there but reward yourself with a break. Stretch, exercise, go for a walk, and then come back and pick up where you left off before the interruption. Different situations require different responses. Knowing that you have choices can help you cope with each situa-tion, enabling you to prevent an uncivilized angry outburst.

One approach that I have found to yield positive results when managing anger is to place distance between yourself and the feeling. Instead of saying "I'm angry," try using "I'm feeling angry right now." The first statement identifies you more closely with the anger. The second gives distance and perspective. Anger is a temporary feeling and emotion that happens in the moment. It is the same when you say, "I'm an angry person" or "People tell me I'm an angry person." These two statements tie you closely to the emotion. To distance yourself, try, "I need to learn to work on the best approach to man-age my anger when it occurs," or "When I feel angry, I don't always behave well towards others. This is an area that I need to improve on."

Another technique that I have found helpful is to learn your own consciousness. What are the things that trigger your anger? Learn the triggers that cause you to become angry. Once you learn and understand what your triggers are, it becomes easier to address and turn off the voices in your head that steers your anger. One of the common sayings in counseling is, "If it is hysterical, it is historical." In other words, the person is not responding to a situation that has just happened. The given situation has triggered a memory or deep-seated emotion, which causes them to react out of all proportion to what has occurred.

Anger will have a devastating effect on your personal life, career, and health unless you learn how to manage it constructively. Anger left to its own demise will destroy you, your family, and others you care about. The potential that anger holds to destroy your life is high, and if you struggle with controlling it, use the techniques I have provided. It is important to note that we need to control our anger and not let it control us. Educate yourself, and if you cannot find an anger management technique that works for you, find professional help to tame your temper and live your best life.

What We Say Can Hurt

A torn jacket is soon mended, but hard words
will bruise the heart of a child.
—Henry Wadsworth Longfellow

Have you ever said something to someone that you wish you hadn't? Has someone ever said something to you that hurt you to your core? Many of us have said things that we wish we had not said, knowing that in the end, our words were hurtful to those we care about. If there are things we say that are hurtful, why do we say them in the first place? Many times, we say things that hurt others because we hurt inside ourselves.

The repetitive process is something we all know too well: someone says something rude to you or about you, someone wrongly accuses you of doing something, or someone says something that puts you on the defensive. You allow yourself to become angry, so you respond without thinking and with the intention of protecting your feelings. You respond in anger, justifying your own feelings and disregarding the offender's. When you do this, you create an emotional connection to the person that hurt you, which keeps your feelings of hurt alive deep in your subconsciousness. Over time, your mind continues to replay the event or what was said until you lash out.

Why does it seem like there are those who spend so much time saying hurtful words rather than kind words? Is it that they really hurt inside, or is it that most of us do not understand how to communicate our feelings? As individuals, as different as we may seem, we are still all wired emotionally the same. Robert Plutchik's theory states there are eight basic human emotions that we all feel: fear, anger, sadness joy, disgust, surprise, trust, and anticipation. It is how we communicate those feelings that separate us.

When someone says something hurtful to you, do you tell them they hurt you? Or that you are feeling hurt? Many will respond with "You hurt me when you said…" The problem in this situation is that you disown responsibility for your feelings when you use the word *you*. To be able to do something about the way you feel, you must own the feeling by using the word *I*. "I hurt" rather than "You hurt me" enables you to take responsibility for your feelings. When you respond with "I hurt when you say those things to me," you create ownership and validation for your feelings. Responding in this manner does not place blame on the other person for the way you feel; rather, it provides feedback to the other person about how you feel because of what they said. If you do not own your feelings, you cannot do anything about them. Responding in this manner can be uncomfortable at first, making it very difficult to communicate and express your emotions. It may even be counter to your belief system that your feelings are better left unacknowledged. Ask yourself how you feel when something hurtful is said to you. Then state how you feel when those things are said, "I hurt when you say things like that to me."

What we say can hurt those we care about. The next time you want to strike with words to even the score or gain a one up, consider what the consequences will be. In Deepak Chopra's book *Ageless*

Mind, Timeless Body, he states that almost all negative feelings such as anger and resentment begin with the emotion of "hurt." He goes on to say that if "hurt" is not resolved or released, it is internalized, eventually resulting in some other emotion. Considering this, it would be easy to suggest that if you fail to let someone know that their harsh words hurt you, eventually, you will do the same thing. Do not hurt the ones you love and care about with your words. Once they are spoken, you can never get them back.

Stand Up to Be Counted

Over the course of my life, I have had to stand up and be counted many times. Bullies come in all shapes and sizes, and I had to face many of them in my lifetime. Some were employers, some I encountered out in the world, some were adults in my community, and others were students when I was a kid. A bully is anyone who pushes others down to keep themselves up and dominant. The bully strives at seeking separation by placing himself apart and above others. They want to be superior, stronger, and otherwise look better than others around them. Bullying doesn't just happen on the playground when growing up. It happens everywhere, at any given time.

Although bullying happens in all walks of life, the effects are most damaging with young people because of the long-term effect bullying can have on an individual's psyche. Young people are developing and forming ideas about who they are. With the development of self-image, young people become insecure and self-consciousness about who they are and how they look. This becomes the fuel that lights the bullies' fire as it gives them power over the individual. Being bullied can create lifelong issues of low self-esteem, depression, anxiety, and poor school performance. It also creates a sense of loneliness as the person being bullied withdraws from social activities.

Bullying goes against everything we are taught at a young age about caring for others. We learn to be hospitable, compassionate, and to look out for one another. By bullying others to obtain self-gain, you become the outlier. You become the asshole that no one likes or wants to be around, leading you to a lonely life. Imagine what your eulogy would be at your funeral. The speaker standing in front of an empty room, "Here lies [enter your name here], the lonely jackass that no one liked because he bullied everyone to gain self-worth." Not a pretty image, is it? When you push people down you do not better yourself, you lessen yourself. Likewise, if you are trying to pull someone up, you are also improving yourself. What you say and do to others will have a long-lasting effect, good or bad, on you as well. You have a choice! Do you want to be the asshole that no one likes, or do you want to be the person that builds others up?

Words are powerful.

- Offensive language—when a bully uses offensive language, they are looking for a reaction.
- Put-downs—when a bully uses a put-down, they do this so they may appear superior to you.
- Payback—when a bully uses a payback, they want to bring you down so they will regain their superiority.

How you counteract bullying does not depend on who the bully is or on the bully's actions but on how you think about yourself, your confidence, and your self-esteem. We do not see people as they are; we see them as we are. If you do not value yourself, you put yourself into the position of becoming the victim of a bully. The higher you value yourself, the more likely you are to stand up to the bully's actions, for yourself and others.

- You are a 10 on a scale of 10
- You are unique
- You are gifted
- You can make the right choices
- You have influence
- You use your influence to help yourself and others

Statistics show, in most instances, if someone says something in the first five seconds, the bully will stop. Everyone wants to be a hero, and you can be the hero by helping someone who is being bullied. The bully is always pushing people down, but the hero is always picking up those around them. Heroes can see what is not right and act accordingly. They are passionate about their stance and feel the need that they must make a change. Bullying itself creates the situation that is ripe for a hero making it an opportunity to be significant. You can be signifiant by

- lifting others up,
- standing up for others,
- picking up others.

Words are a powerful force of both the good and the bad. Sometimes, a bully will use his force to physically attack; however, bullying typically begins with words. Do you remember the old saying "Sticks and stones will break my bones, but words will never hurt me"? The truth is words can hurt; in fact, words can penetrate you like a knife to your chest, seeking out your heart. That is why bullies like to use words rather than force. Words are tools just like a hammer you use to build a house or you use to destroy it. The hammer is just a tool, not inherently good or evil. The choice is up to you on how you use the hammer.

When I was in high school there were three groups of students: the jocks, the nerds, and the freaks. The jocks were the students that were good at sports, the nerds were the students that were smart, and the freaks were the students good at things like art and music. These labels were all designed as "put-downs." Instead of saying, "You are good at basketball," people would say, "You're a jock." Words could have been used to say something good, but words were used to identify an individual as a put-down instead. If someone was smart, people would say, "You're a nerd." The word *nerd* is designed to make people feel bad about being smart and obtaining good grades in class. Can you see how wrong this is? Any language that is designed to offend, put down, or make someone pay is a form of bullying.

We tend to see bullies as the other guy, but...

- have you ever used offensive language towards someone solely for a reaction?
- have you ever used your words to put someone down?

- have you ever used your words to pay someone back? You know, someone hurt you and you are going to make them pay.

All these are a form of bullying. It is also something you need total control over. It is very possible you will not be able to stop someone else from bullying, but you can stop yourself from being the negative impact on others. Instead of using your words to put people down, use your words to help people up. When you feel like saying something negative to somebody, think of something positive to say. Instead of saying, "You're such a nerd," try "You are really smart." Your words are a tool just like a hammer. You can use your words to put people down, or you can use your words to build them up. The Golden Rule: "Do unto others as you would have them do unto you." This phrase is not just a good rule, it is a spiritual law. Whatever you do to people will be done back to you. Use your words to build people up, and others will say kind things to you. Use your words to make a stand that counts.

Positive Self-Image

You fail forward by making each failure you have a learning experience that, in the end, helps you move closer to what you want. Do you believe in this statement? I do. Hold your right hand out in front of you with your palm down. Hold your hand flat like you are making a roof. Now bring your left hand upward to hit it against the roof or "lid." In other words, your right hand is palm down and acting like it is a roof or a lid. Bring your left hand up and have the top side of your left hand smack against the palm of your right hand. This is a symbolic visual image of hitting the lid or the potential you have set for yourself. On a scale of 1 to 10, if your self-image is a 3, then your success in life can only be a 2, and so on. Your right hand represents the 3, and your left hand hitting the palm of your right hand represents a 2. You have hit your potential and can go no higher than a 2. Your self-image is the way you see yourself. Your self-image is the cap on your ability to achieving your success. How important is it? You may succeed if nobody else believes in you, but you will never succeed if you don't believe in yourself. That's how important it is.

The most important conversation you have on any given day is the one that you have with yourself. Coach John Wooden, the winningest college basketball coach of all-time, states, "Don't be concerned with what others think, say, or believe about you; but be concerned with what you think, say, and believe about yourself." Your limiting factor is not what others think, say, and believe; it is what you think, what you say, and what you believe to be true about yourself.

How you see yourself determines how others see you. It is impossible with a low self-image for you to see others in a positive way. If you see yourself as a 6, you will see others as a 6. Even more likely, if you see yourself as a 3, you will see others as a 2. The lower you go on the self-image scale, the more reasons you see others even lower than yourself on that scale. However, if you see yourself as a 9, meaning you are very comfortable with yourself, then you are more likely to feel comfortable surrounding yourself with other 9s and 10s. There is a relationship between comfort level and self-image. The lower you are on the self-image scale, the greater the gap you have between yourself and others on that scale. As one goes higher on the scale, the gap becomes less important. Comfort level can go down in areas of ability, talent, and self-image but cannot elevate.

Another way to look at it is, those at the lower end of the scale have no desire to climb the ladder and surround themselves with the type of people that can make a difference in their lives. They have a challenging time processing it emotionally. They are in their comfort zone. The number on the self-image scale you put on your-self becomes the number that others put on you too. In a sense, it becomes a self-fulfilling prophesy.

The greatest indicator of anyone's future is their self-image. How do you see yourself? There are those who fail to get what they want out of life, which is why it remains a dream. The reason your dreams do not come to fruition is because what you receive from life is directly proportional to how you see yourself in life. A low self-image will sabotage a dream; it will kill it before it is conceived. If you have a positive self-image and a dream, more than likely, you will achieve it. It is not the dream that will be achieved but the self-image. When you tell yourself "I don't think I can do XYZ," it rises from the belief, "I don't think I am XYZ." It is not that the action is unachievable, but it is not believing you can achieve that leads to whatever it is becoming unachievable. The most important part is that a positive self-image does not begin with what we do, nor does it begin with what we have; it begins with who we are. The clothes, the cell phone, and the social media accounts will all go away. When all is gone, what do you have left? For this reason alone, you never want to define yourself by what you have. It is a big mistake to define yourself through your material possessions or how many Facebook followers you have.

Your self-image is how you see yourself. How do you see yourself? When you look in the mirror, what do you see? Do you think positive or negative thoughts about yourself? Are you happy to see yourself? Sadly, there are those who really are insecure and are unhappy to see themselves. A healthy self-image is when you think positive thoughts about yourself and others around you. An unhealthy self-image is the opposite. It is when you think negative thoughts about yourself and others. Your self-image determines how you see yourself and how others see you. If you think you're a badass, others will think the same.

Do you often think things like, "I'm not good at math, so I will never be able to get this job? Might as well not send my resume." If you think this way, then you will never do what it takes to be good at whatever it is you want to achieve. When you go for the interview or take on the challenge, you fail. The failure confirms in your mind that you are not good enough and will not be accepted, and the cycle repeats itself. What if you believe you are good at math and take the time to study before the interview, giving yourself the best possible chance of getting the job you want? Easy enough, right? If you do not do what it takes to be successful, you are confirming in your mind your self-limiting belief that you are not good enough regardless of the fact YOU DIDN'T STUDY, YOU DIDN'T PRACTICE, YOU DIDN'T

PREPARE. Your mind excludes those facts and keeps your self-limiting belief intact, in place ready to repeat itself the next time you go for your next interview. You may have convinced yourself that there are people more qualified than you, so! That does not mean you cannot be the better person for the job. It begins with how you think about yourself. The good news is you can change your self-image. There is a saying, "As a man thinks in his heart, so is he." You are what you think. Start thinking, "I'm the right person for this position." Stop procrastinating and start studying, start practicing. Put in the extra effort to be successful. When your knowledge increases or you can do the math needed at your job, you will feel good about yourself and get accepted. Now you have started a new cycle.

Think positive thoughts about yourself and others. Seek and find what you excel at and focus on it. Attack it! Hang out with people who make you become a better person. Avoid those who push you around and belittle you so they may appear superior.

These seven questions will help you change your perception of yourself in a positive way:

1. What do you like about your life?
2. What people make you feel special and push you to be better?
3. What can you do today that is positive in somebody's life?
4. What positive qualities do you want in your life?
5. What do you do well?
6. What wins have you experienced recently?
7. What are you doing today that will make you better tomorrow?

Your Personal Character

No matter how gifted and talented an individual may be, it is critical to make the right choices. Your personal character is a foundation block for your life that is made up of the choices you make. Every minute of every day, every individual on this planet makes thousands of choices. Personal character is an accumulation of qualities that distinguish us as being dependable and trustworthy or not. These engraved personal qualities are the results of positive or negative choices we make along our journey through life.

The most important part of building character is in understanding how to align your personal values, philosophies, and ethics in a way that enables you to build personal character that is respectable. One of the areas you must align yourself with are personal values. What do you believe? What are your values? You want to align your beliefs with what and how you think. What do you feel? Do your feelings align with your thoughts and beliefs? The last area you need to align is how you act. How do you act? Are your actions ethical? Are your actions aligned with your values, thoughts, and feelings? Values, thoughts, and feelings are essential ingredients in the development of your character; and when you work on aligning these areas, your character blossoms.

Character traits, whether good or bad, are revealed during different events. In a crisis, good character traits will make you determined, and poor character traits will present itself as discouragement. Developing moral and positive character traits is your best insurance policy for managing through the difficult days that may present themselves in the future.

Your character is an accumulation of qualities that make us dependable and trustworthy toward ourselves and others. Qualities like honesty, integrity, and keeping your word are the desired qualities that have a direct impact on how others perceive your dependability, accountability, and trustworthiness. Do your values, thoughts, and feelings align in a way that people see you as an honest person of integrity who they can depend on? Every choice you make during your journey through life will have consequences. Whether good or bad, your choices also determine your character. Many of us lack the positive character that leads us to making the correct choice we need to make. If you do not have character that is positive and ethical, that is your starting point. Your life is the product of the choices you make and the character you carry with you.

Your self-discipline also has a role in determining your character. I hear many people say I just can't win! REALLY? Or is this statement a product of discouragement resulting from poor character? I believe you can win, and the first win you need to work on is victory over yourself. Victory through self-discipline is essential. Discipline bridges the gap between where you are to where you are going. Self-discipline is the engine to determination that powers you toward achieving your dreams when you would have quit long ago. With self-discipline comes sacrifice, and to achieve your dreams, you must give up something of lesser value for the greater gain. If you are not willing to give up your free time for the training needed to advance, YOU DO NOT ADVANCE.

Take a moment to write down the top five character traits you believe are essential when thinking of a good friend. Then think about what type of person they are. What kind of qualities do they have? Now consider the negative traits you discover when you think of a bad friend or acquaintance. When you are finished, the traits you write down for the good friend and the ones you write for the bad friend will differ greatly.

All of us have an inner voice called "conscience." Your conscience knows the difference between right and wrong—or at least it should. But example after example, there are individuals who make you wonder if they have a conscience. Or do they choose not to listen? Have you ever sipped something so hot that it burned your tongue to the point you were unable to taste anything? It's like your tongue becomes numb. Depending on how hot whatever it was you sipped, your tongue could be unable to taste anything for a long time. The same thing can happen to your conscience. If your conscience has become numb because of bad choices, it becomes difficult to know the difference between right and wrong. Your choices determine your character, and your conscience knows the right choice to make so long as you haven't let your conscience go numb. If you listen to your conscience, you will make correct choices that leads to strong character. Is it possible to silence your conscience? I think the answer is YES! The problem is, do we choose to listen?

In any given situation, if you know the right choice but act in a way that is detrimental to yourself or others, negative consequences will result. Simple cause and effect principle. But what if negative consequences do not occur? It becomes easier the next time to act in a negative manner. As the cycle repeats, eventually, your conscience would not speak to you anymore as your inner voice falls on deaf ears. Your conscience has been silenced. You have made a new imprint on your mind that says it is okay to do the wrong thing because there are no negative consequences. The cycle continues to repeat; the negative action is molded into a habitual pattern. The continuous release of dopamine feeds your conscience until the pattern is broken with negative results. Then it's too late. Your choices determine your character, and your character determines the quality of your life. By listening to your conscience, you will make the correct choices. Consider this: your self-discipline determines how strong your character is. Your conscience helps lead you to making the right choice as self-discipline allows you to listen to that inner voice the first time. Be disciplined enough to listen to your conscience so you make the correct choice the first time and not have to reap the negative consequences of the bad choice you have sown.

Doing the wrong thing is easy if you are not caught. Right? Our prisons are filled with people who have made the wrong choice and are living out the consequences locked up behind bars. But many of us make wrong choices daily. Some are not so detrimental as others, but for some people, making wrong choices is an easy choice to make. Doing the right thing involves making tough decisions while using your self-discipline to maintain a positive character. An example of this leads me to a story I heard years ago. An oyster fisherman along the emerald coast of Florida despised starfish. Why? He came to find out starfish enjoyed fishing for oysters just as much as the fisherman. For many years, the fisherman developed a plan that would maximize his oyster production. He believed that if there were less starfish in the gulf, there would be more oysters for the market.

His strategy was when a fisherman caught a starfish, he would pull out a knife and cut the starfish in half and throw both halves back into water. Every September, when oyster season began, he found that there were MORE starfish. The fishermen did not understand what was happening, so they continued to cut the starfish in half and throw them back. The starfish population continued to grow as did the fishermen's frustration. Interestingly enough, one characteristic of starfish is their ability to regenerate. If you take a knife and cut off the leg of a starfish, he grows a new leg. If you cut a starfish in half, you have created two starfish. Since both halves will grow new legs, the starfish population continued to grow, depleting the oyster harvests. Do you think the starfish likes to get cut in half? Even though it is painful for the starfish to get cut in half, the result is better for the starfish.

This story leads me back to what I stated previously about sacrifice. Sometimes, you must sacrifice and give up something to move forward. Sometimes, giving up something of lesser value to gain something of greater value is necessary. Where do you see yourself five years from now? How do you get there? Self-discipline is the bridge that gets you from where you are now to where you are going. Just as the starfish sacrificed themselves and overwhelmed the fisherman, you must do the same for your dreams and goals. The person who has a dream of becoming a doctor may have to give up time with friends or seeing the latest movie. The runner who wants to go to the Olympics will have to spend time on the track and eat the right foods to improve their performance. Only self-discipline will hold you accountable to your goals.

You may be a hard worker, but without a positive self-image, you are sabotaging your efforts. If you have unconditional love and a good self-image but lack self-discipline, you cannot maximize on the positive benefits from the other two areas. If you never learn when you fail, you will continue to fail. If you are not a person of good character, people will never be able to know, like, and trust you. It is your choice to take the information and set yourself on a new course, or you can stay in your comfort zone watching life pass you by.

Commitment

Your personal commitment to success will lead you to victory. Look at your personal commitment as your intention to produce results. We all have good intentions to produce the results we desire. They can be as simple as being on time for an important meeting or as complex as developing a plan for a new business. Your commitment is the bridge between the intentions you envision and the reality of the actions you take. Simply put, what you want and what is. When you think about it, good intentions that become reality is how you use your vision to create a desired reality. Commitment is more than just words; it is more than just the right intentions. Commitment requires action. Without action, reality will continue to be a vision. I have had many great ideas in my life. Some of the them I even acted on, but there have only been a few that I devoted my time and committed myself to. These were the ideas I knew deep down I was willing to do whatever was necessary to make happen. My vision was linked to my reality.

When you are committed to something, you no longer allow yourself to become distracted. You no longer give power to the negative chatter in your head. You become clear and focused about the results you are seeking, and you take the steps that are essential to make it happen. W. M. Murray, in his book *The British Himalayan Expedition*, paints a clear image of this:

> *Until one is committed, there is hesitancy, the chance to draw back, always ineffectiveness. Concerning all acts of initiative and creation, there is one elementary truth the ignorance of which kills countless ideas and splendid plans: that the moment one definitely commits oneself, then providence moves too. All sorts of things occur to help one that would never otherwise have occurred. A whole stream of events issue from the decision, raising in one's favor all manner of unforeseen incidents and meetings and material assistance, which no man could have dreamed would come his way.*

What an amazing statement. Considering what he is implying, commitment applies to everything from extreme life changes to things we face every day. From giving your employer an honest day's work to spending time with your family. In my experience, I have found people who are unable to keep daily commitments are also the same individuals that lack the ability to be accountable while staying committed. How good is your word? Is your word respected? Is your integrity intact? Can people trust your word? Do they believe you will follow through with the commitments you have made? Do you have the discipline to do what you say you will do? Can others count on you? These are all very important questions to ask yourself regarding commitments. The question I think that is most important and is seldom asked is, "Do you understand that the power to achieve lives within you?" You just need to commit.

There are times when we make a commitment and are unable to remain focused. We become sidetracked, and we fail to fulfill the commitment. Life happens, but is this the norm for you or the exception? There is a difference. If life comes at you fast and blocks your commitments, are you honest with yourself and others about your shortcomings? Or do you justify missing the mark by developing excuses and blaming others? It is very possible that the reason you fell short of fulfilling your commitment is because you have a problem completing tasks. Are you putting things off rather than making things happen? Making excuses and blaming others for your broken commitments will lead you to a dead end. It will bring you down with guilt and weakens your ability to make things happen for yourself and others. One action I do when I miss a commitment is I return to the point where I made the commitment. I ask myself, "Was it really a commitment or was it a wish? Was it something I decided on doing on my own, or was it a decision based on trying to please someone else?" When you miss a commitment, be honest with yourself. Own up to it and learn from it. When you take this approach, it forces you to look at the important bullet point rather than the commitment. It makes you consider what might have been lost in translation and where you fell short.

In today's world of entitlement and instant gratification, the idea of commitment is becoming watered down at all levels. I have determined from people I have spoken with along my journey that they do not fully understand or appreciate the importance of living up to their commitments. Many miss the point or lack the understanding of how important it is to follow through on commitments they make. Commitment is a long-term promise you make with yourself and others to fully dedicate yourself to your task, your training, and your team. This promise becomes especially important when adversity is met along the way. The key point to commitment means investing the necessary effort and actions to make something happen by action, not by a verbal promise. Here are the six important points I believe are the foundation to a serious commitment:

1. *Solemn promise.* Instead of just casual talk and meaningless words, you make a solemn pledge to yourself and others. When you create and adhere to this pledge, you fully understand the consequences of your commitment. When I joined the Navy, I made a solemn pledge to support and defend our country. When I married my wife, I made a solemn promise to her until death do us part.

2. *Full investment.* When you make a serious commitment, you fully invest yourself in the cause mentally, physically, and emotionally. You are completely connected to the cause. You give full attention, energy, and effort focused on the goal.

3. *Sacrifice.* You are willing and ready to make personal sacrifices for the commitment even if it causes personal hardship. Commitment means you knowingly and willingly give up aspects of your life that you might want in the short-term to potentially have substantial gain in the long-term.

4. *Long-term obligation.* Serious commitments are long-term obligations you must continually work toward with the intent to see it through to completion. A long-term commitment is not something that you try before you buy or test the water before you jump into the pool. A long-term commitment is something that you establish, something you embody, and something you embrace for the long haul.

5. *Pact to persevere.* Something you stick with even when—and most importantly when—the going gets tough, "for richer or poorer, in sickness and health." When you make

a commitment to someone or something, you are making a pact to persevere through the hardships together. Serious commitment is not always easy, but I have found that it is always worth it.

6. ***Agreement to act***. The most important part to any commitment is your action. Your agreement to act on a commitment is only realized through your actions on a regular basis. Your commitment and character will be measured by your actions, by your deeds.

When making a commitment, there are no gray areas of action. You either act or you don't. You commit yourself and your time or you withdraw. Anyone that is quick to throw in the towel and quit when the going gets tough will not be successful. Commitment has been a powerful force in my life. I am committed to my family, my friends, my work. The greatest commitment in my life has been and always will be the solemn promise to my wife; we have been married for more than forty-one years. I consider myself deliberate in my acts of service and kindness. My level of commitment has provided me power in business as an important member of the team. I show up on time for meetings, I complete assignments, and I respect others. These are all commitments I have made to myself to live up to.

I have met many people who walk through life going through the motions of being committed, but they fail at it. They do not stay true to themselves and lack the discipline to remain committed to the team. As I hold others accountable, I hold myself accountable for the commitments I make. When you live up to your commitments, you become a powerful person of influence. You become a person of your word, remaining accountable to your words and actions; what you say is what you do.

Are you completely honest with yourself when considering if you are as committed to X as you lead on to be? Are you all in, or do you make commitments only to break them and then justify your actions with excuses? The hardest question of all is are you committed enough to yourself to take the actions needed to be known as a person of your word? Are you a person who lives up to their commitments? As the old saying goes, your actions speak louder than your words.

Hard Work

During one of my radio shows, I interviewed my youngest son, Brian, who is a doctor of physical therapy. He shared health tips and discussed the training he endures for obstacle course racing. What he did not share during the interview is that many of the races he signs up for, he usually runs twice on race day. Back-to-back course completions with no breaks. Each lap is twelve miles long while overcoming difficult obstacles along the way. So, while everyone else is running twelve miles, he is running twenty-four miles total on any given race day. The training he endures takes commitment, dedication, and hard work. Have you ever felt like the universe is working against you while others seem to get all the big breaks? This group of people always seem to be the lucky ones as they find themselves at the right place at the right time. While it may appear to be true that others get all the breaks, it is also true that we can all do more to create our own breaks. For many of us, the problem is getting our ass off the couch long enough to dedicate ourselves to task or goal.

Have you been passing up opportunities to gain experience through extra training because that extra training is scheduled after work hours? Have you passed up chances to try something new because you allowed your nervousness and anxiety to gain the best of you? Maybe it is time for you to roll up your sleeves and work a little harder or longer. Ever thought of that concept? It is a great concept! Maybe it is time for you to do your own personal obstacle race. Maybe it is time for you to start creating your own opportunities at work and in your personal life. Have you thought about what steps you need to take to make whatever it is you want a reality? Anything worth having will take effort or, in other words, *hard work*. Maybe it is hard work you are afraid of or lack of a work ethic. How bad do you want whatever it is that you want?

I remember a story my dad told me when I was a child. It was about hard work and turning points that I would experience in my life. The story was about one of my favorite baseball players, Mickey Mantle. Mickey Mantle was the son of a miner from Oklahoma. His father introduced him to baseball at an early age, and even though Mickey was a great baseball player, he struggled when he entered Major League Baseball. Due to his struggles with the New York Yankees, he was sent down to their farm team in Kansas City where he went 0 hits for 22 at bats. This was the worst batting slump of his career. One night, he called his father, saying, "I don't think I can play baseball anymore." The next morning his father appeared unannounced in Mickey's hotel room and started packing a suitcase. As his father jammed Mickey's clothes into the suitcase, Mickey asked what he was doing. His father responded, "You're going home. You're going to work in the mines, that's what we're doing. You can work back down there." Needless to say, Mickey did not work in the mines, and he bounced back from his batting slump, hitting .360 for Kansas City and returning to the Yankees. Looking back years later, Mickey Mantle said, "That was the turning point in my life."

Your turning point is the moment you take that first step toward an opportunity that could change your life. That first intentional step toward what you want takes effort and hard work. It is not so much a physically hard step, but it will be something mentally tough that you will have to overcome.

Hard work does pay off in many ways, but the biggest way is through the results of the consistent application of effort. You must be dedicated to your effort. Dedication to effort is the very essence of hard work. One of the most important things I have learned over my years about hard work is that you cannot fake it. Hard work is necessary in just about everything you do; it cannot be circumvented, skipped, or artificially accelerated. You must put in the work and the time. This does not mean that alternative solutions are not available; they are, but even alternative solutions require a dedicated effort to get things done. As far back as I can remember, my grandparents, parents, teachers, and coaches have told me that if I work hard enough, I can and will achieve anything. I have come to accept this as a life truth. Over the years, my wife and I have shared this truth with our children and now with our grandchildren. We all feel like we are working hard, but for some of us, it seems like we are in quicksand, slowly sinking the harder we try. THIS IS NOT TRUE! The simple act of starting the process of going after what you want moves you down the path of success and one step closer to your goal.

Five factors that all hard work should include the following:

DRIVE—The motivation, the inspiration, the reasoning of why you work hard. It is the push behind your efforts. It is the heart of your effort.

PLAN—The course of action. Your plan is the map to your success. It is the "how" behind your drive to success.

SACRIFICE—Sacrificing is the tangible and intangible items you give up when you work hard. Hard work requires personal sacrifice and enduring the strain on relationships and finances so you may succeed. Sacrifice will truly test your comfort level.

GRIND—The grind is the dedication to the sacrifices you make. When everything stops being fun and glamorous, it is your grind that pushes you through. How you handle the GRIND separates the winners and quitters.

PAYOFF—This is the brass ring, the grand prize. The pay-off is the end product of your drive, plan, sacrifice, and grind.

Hard work is a chosen lifestyle. Stay driven toward your plan, accepting the sacrifices along the way. As you grind through the tough times, the payoffs will start to arise. Take the payoffs, celebrate your wins, and then reinvest your wins into your next challenge. It has taken hard work to write this book and many hours of dedication, but even though it has been difficult, every minute of it has been fun, exciting, and challenging. This has given me a profound sense of accomplishment and purpose. When you work hard, take risks that scare you, and attack them, you will achieve notable goals along the way. Your PAYOFF is not only monetary rewards but the internal personal satisfaction you experience that cannot be described in words. The only way to know how it feels is to experience it. What hard work do you have ahead of you? What hard work have you been putting off? Now is the time to take on the tasks and work hard toward achieving them.

Choices You Make

Take a moment to think about the choices you have made in your life. As you sit thinking about them, do you wish you hadn't made some of those choices? I have made choices my whole life. Some I am proud of, others not so much. With each choice I have made, there were consequences that I had to live with.

A few years ago, on the front page of a New York newspaper, there was a photograph of a person who had fallen to the subway tracks below. The photograph was taken just before an approaching train hit and killed this person. The photographer made a choice when he took that photograph of the person struggling to get out of the way of the approaching train. In no more than a click of his camera shutter, the photographer placed more value toward a photograph rather than a life. When I saw the photograph, it got me thinking about the photographer and the family of the person killed. How many other people, family members, and friends will also suffer the consequences of that one camera click? How does the photographer feel knowing in the time it took for him to click his camera's shutter, a person lost their life?

The choices we make define who we are, and they affect not only ourselves but so many others as well. I wonder if the roles were changed, would the photographer have wanted the individual to take the picture or to help save him from the approaching train. Personally, I live by the Golden Rule that was ingrained in me many years ago. Treat others in the same way you want to be treated. When interacting with people, you have a choice to treat people the way you want to be treated, or you can choose to photograph the moment a life is taken by an approaching train. It is your choice that only you can make.

Have you ever asked yourself, "Is this right for me? "Decision-making. Choices. Options. Personal judgments. Doing the right thing. All these phrases have one thing in common. That is, you are trying to determine if something you are considering is right for you. We make choices every day, but is it the right one? We make a choice on whether we will ride the bus or ride our bicycle. We choose between foods on a menu. We choose who our friends are or who we want to date. We choose whether to apply for a job or to change our career path. Choose whether to send out our resume to potential employers or be content where we are. Or we choose to click a camera shutter just as a life is taken.

There are times when making a choice is not as easy as deciding between menu items at your favorite restaurant. Making business or relationship decisions can have a profound effect on your life for years to come. You want to make the right choice for yourself, but how will it affect your life journey and the people around you? How do you decide if something is right for you? Do you go with your instinct, or do you create a "pros and cons" list of why? What if that doesn't work, then what? Everyone wants to make the best choices and know that they are the right decisions for themselves. Unfortunately, life is not that simple.

Whenever I talk about choices, people ask me, "How do I know if a decision is right for me?" Making the right decision can feel like you are being pulled in many directions. When you do decide, you are not even sure it is the right choice. You begin second-guessing yourself and the choice you made. This leads to negative chatter and thoughts in your head as the battle of the "what-if" begins. Your inner voices go into attack mode, destroying your positive, motivated self. Do yourself a favor and learn how to trust your decisions and remain positive and motivated as you see them through.

The problem I see is that people do not like or want to be held responsible for the choices they make. Most times, people do not want to admit that their choices have real-life consequences. When making your choice, it may seem possible, but you cannot escape the consequences of your decisions, whether good or bad. Once you make your choice, the results of that choice are unavoidable. People think if they make a poor decision, there will be someone there in a knight costume, waiting to rescue them. Life seems like a fairy tale to them, but that is not the case.

What we fail to understand is the choices we make have created everything in our lives, and we fail to claim responsibility for the life we have created. To move forward and into a successful, fulfilling life, you need to give up blaming and complaining about your life and take full responsibility for it. Once you acknowledge every experience in your life has been created by you, it becomes possible to take charge of creating the life you want.

Everything you experience today is a direct result of choices you have made in the past. Lou Holtz, the only football coach in NCAA history to lead six different college teams to postseason bowl games, emphasizes this point, "The man who complains about the way the ball bounces is likely the one who dropped it." You must choose to stop blaming and complaining so you can personally move forward. Jack Canfield, the author of *Chicken Soup for the Soul*, says, "The bottom line is that you are the one who is creating your life the way it is. The life you currently live is the result of all of your past thoughts and actions." If you believe what Jack Canfield states, then you believe you can control your thoughts and feelings going forward. With this belief, you can control what goes on in your mind. You can control what you put into your mind, what you read, what you watch on TV and at the movies and the people you hang out with. Every action, every choice, every decision you make is under your control. When put in that perspective, to be more successful, "all you have to do is act in ways that produce more of what you want."

If you have not already, it is time for you to take 100 percent responsibility for your life, the choices you have made, and the results you have produced. It is 100 percent your choice to procrastinate and put things off until tomorrow. People who fail to achieve success in pursuing their dreams, almost without exception, fail to make choices and decisions in a timely manner. That is if they can make choices and decisions at all. Your life is not made by the dreams you dream but by the choices you make about the dreams you have. Think about how the choices you have made have changed your life up to this point. We can all look back to different events and choices we have made that had a profound effect on the path we have taken. You might even consider writing some of them down and reflect on them. Reflection about the choices you have made and how they alter your life journey is key. Learning from your past so you can move forward in the future is a choice you want to make. Reflection on how opportunities were either missed or how you hit the target with the right choice is vital in self-development.

Our ability to make choices gives us the power to direct the course our life takes. We also make the choice of what type of person we want to be and what actions we will make to grow into that person. Contrary to popular beliefs, we are not the result of how our parents raised us or a product of our environment. We are solely a result of the choices we make daily.

A few years ago, I spoke at several correctional institutions in Oregon. During one of my presentations, a young man stood up and stated, "Yeah, it's all so easy for you to say. You are successful, and I am locked up in here." I said to him, "The only difference between you and me are the choices we have made. With the wrong choice, I too could have easily been locked up somewhere. It truly is all about choices." During this same trip, I also visited several substance abuse rehabilitation centers where the individuals I spoke with had more than their fair share of excuses. Many of them blamed everyone else for their substance abuse, and for some, accepting responsibility for their addictions was difficult. One individual told me, "You just don't get it, choice ain't the reason I'm here. The man put me in here." After digesting this response from him, I said, "It has everything to do with choice. The first time you stuck a needle in your arm, snorted a line of coke, or popped a handful of pills in your mouth, it had everything to do with the choice you made at that moment. Making that choice put you here. It has affected your family, your friends, and your life all because of a simple choice you made."

To achieve success, it is important to know how to determine if you are making the right choices. I have found that when I pay attention to my intuition, I often make the right choice. Sometimes, making the right choice comes down to listening to what your instinct is telling you. Intuitive guidance, meditation, following your heart, and gaining clarity by listening to your instincts are all forms of intuition. Leave your emotional reactions out of the process of contemplating your choice. You should have sudden clarity, not anxiety, when it is your instinct speaking. Although your intuition is always an important source, using rational thinking and seeing something from a different view is just as important in making the right decision. Take time to weigh the pros and cons of each choice before acting. You need to consider how each decision might affect you realistically. There should be a good balance between your emotional responses and the logical factors.

When you make the right decision, you do not have any regrets or shame in following your choice. Your actions will not affect others in a negative or harmful way and will bring good consequences. Making the wrong decision will usually coincide with second-guessing everything you do related to your action. On the other hand, if you are struggling to decide between what you want and what you feel you should do, consider how you might feel about yourself after you have made the decision. Is it in line with the kind of person you want to be?

Many times, when there is a big decision to make, such as breaking off a relationship or changing jobs, people do not take the time to consider the real cause of why they want to make that change. We tell ourselves stories about the potential benefits of the decision. We think we want to take a new job in a different city as the idea of adventure and excitement is appealing. However, we fail to really look at why we are even considering the idea of changing jobs and moving. Is it because we are bored or have not made friends where we are currently? Or is there a deeper reason?

When we are faced with making a crucial decision, our body becomes stressed. Some may even find it difficult to sleep or eat. The same happens when we make a wrong decision. If you are tense or feeling anxious when you think about a decision you have made, it is possible you are following the wrong choice. On the other hand, if your body feels relaxed, you sleep well, and are excited when you talk about your decision, then you have most likely made the right one. Tune into the physical clues your body is giving you as it may help you connect to the unconscious feelings you have about a choice you are considering. Knowing you made the right decision comes from listening to your body, following your instincts, and weighing the options.

What do you do when you have two choices, and they both seem to be right for you? How do you figure out the right choice? First, take fear out of the equation. Fear is a great motivator for indecision and will prevent you from choosing an action. In your head, you have all these negative "what-if" questions. Your fear in deciding could be whether you can manage life on your own outside the current relationship you are in. "What if I try and fail? What would I do then? How will I be able to make it on my own?" Flip the questions to, "What if I try and succeed? What if I managed on my own and figured it out along the way? What if I jump and build my wings on the way down? What if I am able to make it on my own?"

When it comes to making big decisions, why do you not trust yourself to make the correct choice? You will not always know you are headed in the right direction, but having faith in yourself to make the correct decision is key. Making the right choice will not always happen. You will also make the wrong choices along the way. Learn from those wrong choices and move on. The more information you have on the choices you need to make, the better you are prepared to make the right choice. Many people seek out the advice of trusted friends who have lived through similar situations and can offer alternative views. Beware—seeking out different friends for advice can end in conflicting advice, only confusing you more about the choice you need to make.

It is easy to get lost when trying to make the right decision, which can lead you to total indecision. The best thing you can do when you are not sure what the right choice is for you is to act. Do something! This might mean doing more research, considering other options, or learning to let go of your fear. Acting keeps you moving forward and headed in the right direction. When it comes to making the right decisions, you must know how. It can be very hard to choose the right thing, so take time to think about what you are doing before you do it. Think about the results and consequences while refraining from making any rash decisions. Doing something because it feels right in the moment can lead to bad choices. Take time, at least a few days, to really be sure about what you want. Insignificant things that will not affect your life in a major way require small, quick decisions. The important decisions, like a job change, ending a relationship, or buying a house are bigger decisions that require more thought.

You have probably heard it before: follow your passions and let your passions help you make good decisions. But what if you do not know who you are or what your passions are? How do you get to know yourself so you can make better choices? To experience peace, you need to live in harmony with your true self. When you know who you are and what you want out of life, you are prepared to make better choices. Understanding your own personality will help you be confident in making correct choices on decisions that need to be made. Ask friends what they think your personality is. Dig into your own feelings and knowledge about your personality. Your private personality might be different from your public one. Understand who you are and who you are not. When faced with a situation, ask yourself, "Why did I respond this way?"

Core values are the fundamental beliefs that guide you and play a role in dictating your behavior. They help you understand the difference between right and wrong. Dig deep into your core values to fully understand your personal moral code and the principles you live by. Think about what your top 7 to 10 core values are. These are the ones that play the biggest roles in your decision making, how you communicate, and your day-to-day activities. Which of these values will you never compromise? Is it honesty, integrity, or security? Do you value financial comfort, wisdom, responsibility, or loyalty? Take time to write down your core values, especially the ones you will never compromise.

Know your body's abilities, limitations, flexibility, and balance. Knowing your body's abilities and limitations will help guide you toward the type of challenges you can take on. Explore your dreams and the hopes you have for your future. Knowing them will help you make the correct choices for the type of life you desire. If you want to become a writer, ask yourself what type of writing you want to do. How proficient are you at writing, and can you improve? Are you willing to dedicate a substantial portion of your life to be a writer? Your dreams should be part of every decision you make, especially the important ones. Get to know your strengths and weaknesses, your likes and dislikes, and your quirks and perks. Doing so will provide you with the confidence to make correct decisions on everything. Your likes, dislikes, strengths, and weaknesses are what make you unique, and acting on them will provide you with guidance.

Most importantly, trust your instincts and have faith in yourself. You instinctively know what is best for you, and this will help guide your choices toward making a correct decision. Spend time thinking about each choice you must make and exploring how each outcome would feel to you. Does it bring joy? Are you comfortable with the outcome? Or are you ashamed and embarrassed to share it with others? Making decisions that are right for you depends on your values and how the decision will affect your life and those around you. Do not second-guess yourself. Knowing who you are and what you want to do with your life helps you make better choices in the end.

How You Think

Have you ever wondered how some people succeed where others fail? Much of their success depends on the way they think. Your thoughts turned into words that ultimately drive actions is what defines you. To achieve your desires, you must have a mindset that overcomes the challenges that will distract you from your desired goal. Do not let your life be shaped by the beliefs and words of others but rather by your own. Those with a mindset that overcomes, understand that words are like seeds that have potential to grow and produce fruit. If the seeds planted are dormant, nothing will be produced. If you do not tend to your crop frequently, pests will arrive. If you plant weeds, you produce weeds; plant apples and you will produce apples.

Our minds are shaped by past experiences and by the words that have been spoken throughout our lives. These words have been planted in our minds, have taken root, and now control our lives. You need to guard your mind. Words are like crops in a farm field. When planted in your mind, they will grow and blossom. When these planted seeds are watered, they can grow to empower you, they can debilitate you, and they can even destroy you. They either promote you or demote you. They either become your greatest asset or biggest liability.

I believe words have enormous power. They create images in our mind that allow us to visualize and understand. Whatever you visualize will materialize. People who overcome great obstacles surround themselves with people of the same persona because they understand the power of influence that others have on them. You become the average of the five people you spend the most time with. Knowing this will help you understand how impactful the words from others are on your mind. If you desire to rise above the level of your self-image, you must not let the limiting beliefs of other people hold you back. The person you see in the mirror is what you have created, but for some, the person they see is what they have allowed others to create.

Thoughts are POWERFUL, and with them, you create desires that result in actions. Whether productive or not, actions produce habits. Habits define an individual's character and will deliver them to their desired destination in life. If words have the power to invoke our emotions and our feelings, the habits that derive from them will guide us in our decision making.

Looking back to a defining moment in my life, I remember back to the morning in December 1979 that would change my life forever. I remember being taken by my shoulders and told, "I know you can do this." That morning, two of my close friends were killed. Nine others were wounded in a terrorist attack. I remember being frozen as time stood still. Looking back, I remember thinking about having to jump from a helicopter running for cover, hoping I was not going to be next. I remember, in this moment, imagining my wife and son standing over my coffin with United States flag being draped over it. I remember vividly imaging the tears rolling down their faces as the box I now lay in was being lowered six feet down to rest. Snapping to, I returned to the present moment. The other person I was began preparing his gear to ready himself for a secondary attack. This was the moment when my supervisor grabbed me by the shoulders and planted those words of expectancy, "I know you can do this." I did the job that needed to be done that day and over the days that followed. Little did I know the effect these words would have on me.

From that December morning in 1979 to 1993, I slowly withdrew myself as I continued to spiral down into despair. I grew to be a mean, angry drunk man who was angry at the world. One day in 1993, I sat on my bed, thinking do I go on or do I end the pain and sorrow that I have deep within? It was in this moment when those words I heard long ago flooded back into my mind, "I KNOW YOU CAN DO THIS." Once again, the power of those words saved me. I received the help I needed, I stopped drinking and changed my life. It is said that "we are not the product of our circumstances, we are only the product of our decisions," which is why you must decide to live life to its fullest and surround yourself with the people who will supply you powerful words when you need them most.

Overcoming obstacles in life is not easy to endure. If overcoming obstacles or changing your life was easy, everyone would be doing it, right? It is hard to change your life because change is not an easy thing for us humans to process. Change takes work, and many of us do not want to take the time or effort to do so. The work that change creates results in the personal responsibility for what needs to be done. You are the only one who can make a difference in your life. Life will present challenges that will stretch you and push you in ways that will improve your inner self. I have learned through experience that it is not the talent or education that will provide you the energy to endure life's challenges but rather the EFFORT you put forth that will make the difference. It's simple: no effort input, no result output. I honestly believe that "even *the smallest of efforts will have results.*" One question that always comes to mind when I consider effort is, "Are my positive thoughts matching up with the effort I am putting out?" Are you willing to give up your comfortable thoughts to endure painful hardships that require effort? What will you give up to get through the obstacles that keep you from reaching the mountaintop?

When you figure out what you really want in life, you must align your thoughts with your effort. And when it comes down to it, are you willing to spend the rest of your life going after it? Your time is here and now, but the only way you are going to make it to the top, the only way you overcome the obstacles in your way, is to stop the negative chatter in your head. Start right here and now by thinking positive about what you desire most. By doing this, your actions and efforts will follow so you can do the things needed to change your life. Act on the things that are needed to get you to the summit. There is no doubt that there are scenarios and situations that occur that we cannot control—shit happens. The only thing you should be worried about controlling is yourself and how you think. The things we do, the time we waste, the effort we do not put out are all aspects that can change our lives. If this is so, why do some of us do such a poor job at controlling it?

As I stated earlier and cannot emphasize enough, the one area in your life that you have the power to control is what and how you think. Once you understand *"what you think is what you become,"* you become careful about what you think about and how you act on your thoughts. Experts tell us that we are only using between 1 percent and 5 percent of our real potential, which means we are giving, at the most, 5 percent of ourselves to our work, our families, our friends, or on improving ourselves. This also means we are only experiencing at the most 5 percent of the fun, the possibilities, or rewards we could be receiving. Don't allow your thoughts to take you to places you do not want to be and silence the negative thoughts that try to dominate your day.

Success is defined as the progressive realization of a worthy idea. When considering success in this way, it becomes easy to assume that any person who knows what they are doing or where they are going in life is a successful person. This also means the person working two jobs to pay their bills and is attending college working toward a degree is just as successful as any other human being. On the other hand, the person who is not progressively working toward a goal can also be considered unsuccessful as well.

If such a simple definition of success holds true, then why aren't there more successful people? You would think it would be easy, but surveys show that as much as 95 percent of the people surveyed did not consider themselves successful. As many as nineteen out of twenty people did not know why they do the work they do except to earn a paycheck. Such a sad way to live. The problem with this lifestyle is the constant struggle of playing a game that the player is unable to win. It is called "follow the follower." Their thought process was hijacked and manipulated to believe, "Well, if they are doing it, I guess I should too." They have a go-with-the-flow mentality as they drag through life following the "leader" without checking references, without asking questions, and without giving any thought to what they are doing. The easiest way to change your life is to ask yourself this question, "Are the people I am following going where I want to go, and does their ideology match my own?"

From the moment we are born, we are surrounded by people who are reinforcing our minds with information they think we need. Over time, we learn to think, act, and speak like these people. When we enter grade school, we want to be liked and be friends with the other students, so we do everything we can to fit in and find a sense of belonging. So, we begin to follow. This goes on throughout our school years, shaping us into a composite of all the students we spent the most time with. We thrive off the glimmer of hope that someday, we will be like the leaders. After graduating high school, many of us will transition to college or enter the military. This places additional demands to conform and follow. After finishing, we return home to fit in, get a job, and support a family. Many times, we return to a job we had before we left. Or we utilize our networking abilities and find someone who can help us find a job where they work. Once at the new job, we observe the other workers, and we follow their work ethic and flow in the workplace.

Over time, we fall into the same pattern that everyone else has created in the workplace. Consider this: most people put in forty hours a week at their work place. This gives you eighty free hours per five-day workweek. During the eighty hours of free time, many of us will do virtually nothing due to the mental and physical exhaustion stemming from our job. Our mind convinces us that we are tired, and the routine quickly becomes wake up, get ready, go to work, return home, eat dinner, watch X number of hours of TV, go to sleep, and repeat. This cyclic lifestyle will last for the next forty years or until you retire. Once you retire, all that is left is watching your favorite TV shows. Many might think there is nothing wrong with this lifestyle, but I believe there is. Remember, words are seeds that, when planted, will produce an outcome. The problem with this hypothetical story of your life is that you never found out who you were or what your true potential was over the many years of hard work. You never questioned what your true potential or abilities might have been. You never learned the fact that you could have accomplished anything you set your mind to. Instead, you became just like the others as you became cemented in the "follow the followers" game.

What is needed is a paradigm shift in the way we think. What you think is what you become. If you think the same way as others, you will follow the rest of the cattle to the slaughterhouse. Understand that your mind works for you and against you. Once you understand how powerful your mind is, you will begin to act on your potential and create the necessary changes. If what we think we become, take the time to do so. Imagination is everything, and we can become what we imagine.

You Become What You Think

Many people never realize the success they want because they have become the mediocre result of their thoughts. Have you ever thought about why that is? Are you a visionary or a follower?

There's a simple reason why people fail to realize the success they want; they are unable to envision it. People resist—rather refuse—to make the changes needed in their lives to achieve the success they want. Their focus remains on what they must give up rather than all the things they will gain. They fail to realize that everything happens for a reason, and it is the reason that brings the change to their life. Instead, people question, "WHY ME?" or "WHY DOES THIS ALWAYS HAPPEN TO ME?" Sometimes, change hurts; it is uncomfortable, and it requires risk that few are willing to take. Let's face it: people do not enjoy failing, and by taking risk, the chance of failure increases. In the end, the ones who do take the risk, experience the pain and hardships are the ones that successfully muscle through the challenging times. It's true, hardship is a part of the process. Taking risks and enduring hardship is where the biggest gains in life are made.

While considering the many moments I have experienced in my life, I have come to realize that many of those moments have changed the course of my life significantly. Looking back to the December day that my life changed significantly, I can remember the day and moments vividly. The smells, the colors, the sounds, what I was wearing, what others were wearing, what the weather was like, and how I felt are ingrained in my memory. I have realized that at that moment, it never occurred to me that everything would be different moving forward and my life would never be the same again.

I have spoken at many events regarding success and living life intentionally, and each time I speak, my message resonates differently with the many different audiences. Many times after I speak, someone will approach me and tell me, "What you are saying is all well and good, BUT…you don't understand what it is to hurt like me. You don't understand what it is to…" YOU CAN FILL IN THE BLANK. After I digest their statement, I always respond with, "You are right, I do not understand what it was like for you." When you truly ponder their statement, you may understand what the other individual has been through, but you are unable to emotionally connect with their situation.

I say the things I say because I know through my life experiences what it feels like to have people despise and hate me. I know what it feels like to be shot at by people whose sole purpose is to kill me as I try to hide with no place to run. I know what it feels like to be covered in molten sulfur and wake up in a hospital burn unit with the most excruciating pain with nothing except being put into a comatose state to relieve the pain. And I know what it is like to screw up so badly that it brings you to the edge of losing everything meaningful in your life.

Yes, life is hard and, at times, will appear to be unfair. Yes, life at times can be full of pain. In the end, you must put those things behind you. In your head, you must create a positive mind-set that enables you to continue believing that you can move forward with the hard work and heavy lifting needed to live a successful life. Earl Nightingale defines *success* as the "progressive realization of a worthy ideal." I believe the reason so many people do not reach the success they want in their life is conformity. People conforming to the ideals of their peers without considering why and perhaps even knowing where they are going in life.

Think about all the people over sixty-five years old living in our society today. Many are financially struggling as they live below the national poverty line. We say, "Look at them, they worked all their life with nothing to show for it." Most are dependent on social security or someone else for life's necessities.

Consider this:

- We learn to read by the time we are six years old.
- We learn to make a living by the time we reach twenty-five. In my case, I was making a living and supporting a family by that age.
- And yet by the age sixty-five, we have not learned how to become financially independent in the most prosperous country the Earth has ever known.

I personally find an issue with this. Much of the reason for this way of life is that people would rather just conform to what society tells them rather than creating their own destiny. They believe their lives are shaped by inevitable circumstances and external forces they cannot control.

A survey was taken where people were asked two questions regarding their purpose. These questions were, "Why do you work?" and "Why do you get up in the morning?" Of the people surveyed, nineteen out of twenty people had no idea. When really pressed for a response, they answered, "Everyone goes to work in the morning."

It is because everyone else is doing it. How about you? If everyone was jumping off a three-hundred-foot bridge, would you follow? I wouldn't. Have you asked yourself honestly why you go to work in the morning? What is so important in your life that it gets you up and out of bed in the morning?

Take a moment to once again think about the definition of *success.* The only people who succeed are those who are progressively working toward a worthy ideal. It is the one who says, "I am going to become… [fill in the blank]" who has begun working on realizing success.

Successful people are

- the people who realized their sole purpose in life is to be a positive influence as a schoolteacher.

- the women who are stay-at-home moms because their passion is to be the best moms they can be.
- the men who own corner stores because it has been their dream to own their own corner store.
- the entrepreneurs who have ideas that start their own company because it has always been their dream.

Anyone who is deliberately pursing their dreams by their own deliberate choice is considered a success. What are you DELIBERATELY NOT pursuing that, if you acted now, you could change your life? There are so few who deliberately pursue their dreams that there really is not much competition. The only real competition you face is yourself. Think what the outcome could be if you stopped competing with your own limiting beliefs and just started creating possibilities that you act on.

People who become successful tend to grow in their success. Those who believe they are failures continue to fail. The difference: successful people have goals that get them to their dreams. People with goals know where they are headed. They create a positive thought process that drives their ambitions. Unsuccessful people believe life is shaped through circumstances and the events that happen to them brought on by external forces. It has nothing to do with the amount of times you can get back up after getting knocked down. It has everything to do with what you do after getting back up that defines the difference in individuals. IT IS THAT SIMPLE.

THE POWER OF YOUR THOUGHTS GIVES YOU THE POWER TO CHANGE YOUR LIFE IMMEDIATELY. REMEMBER, "WE BECOME WHAT WE THINK ABOUT."

Ralph Waldo Emerson said, "A man is what he thinks about all day long." In the Bible, Mark 9:23 states, "'If you can'? said Jesus. 'Everything is possible for one who believes.'" What do you believe about yourself? What is it that you think about all day long? Are you thinking about your successes or your failures? Are you thinking about all the possibilities for success or all the reasons why you will fail? Whether you believe it or not, whether you understand it or not, "YOU ARE IN THE DRIVER'S SEAT." "We become what we think about." If you truly believe this, you will succeed. Our minds are like planting fields. The land does not care. It will produce poison just as it will produce abundant crops, dependent only on what you sow. If you plant seeds of success in your mind, you will succeed. If you plant seeds of confusion, misunderstanding, fear, and anxiety, you will fail. What seeds are you planting?

Is Fear Holding You Back?

Is fear holding you back? When you hear this, what comes to mind?

A few years ago, I was called into my boss's office. When I entered his office, he closed the door behind me. "Have a seat," he said. "I have an opportunity for you that I would like to share." Immediately, my mind began to race as I began to think of all the opportunities that awaited me. That was when he said to me, "The CEO and I think you would enjoy an early retirement." I was stunned and completely taken off guard. "Nice, but are there any other opportunities you think I might be better suited for?" I responded. Very bluntly he said, "No, not unless you would rather be laid off."

Of course, I took the first choice. Once again, I found myself at a crossroad. I had a choice to make, and I chose the one best suited. At this point, I could let fear take over, or I could continue pushing forward being intentional with living my life. I thought about Robert Frost's poem, "The Road Not Taken" and the last few lines of that poem that I related most with "Two roads diverged in a wood, and I, I took the one less traveled by and that has made all the difference."

The path everyone walks down is much easier than the trail less travelled. It would have been easy for me to let fear take hold of me and retreat to my comfort zone. It would have been easy to allow fear to take control of every action as I accepted my fate of early retirement. To some, early retirement is not such a bad deal; but not for me, it would have been easy to have been consumed with worries of how I was going to make it. What about my bills, what will people say, what will my wife say, what do I tell my family and friends...?

Over the years, I have learned that channeling your fears in a positive way takes effort, courage, commitment, and a spiritual awakening. I have come to realize that everyone has setbacks, that everyone will fail at least once in their life journey. I have also found that it is what you do when you get back up after being knocked down that will define who you are and what the rest of your life will be like.

After that morning of opportunity, I realized there are plenty of people who believe they know what is best for your life. They want to share their life journey and how they responded to a similar scenario. They want you to take their advice on how you should be living your life. When I decided to live my life on my terms, I decided early that I would not listen to the nonsense advice people provided me. Most of the advice was given out of their own fears. Life is too good, life is too short, and life is too rewarding to listen to advice that is based in fear. Besides, if you live by the advice from others, you will find that you are not living your own life. You end up living a life of conformity as you follow the path that others have made with the same ideas, standards, and beliefs.

"Why would I want to change just to conform to someone else's idea of what would make me happy?" A question I struggled to answer as a young person. As I progress through life, I have come to realize that if I was truly going to live my life on my own terms, why would I wait until I retire before I started enjoying life? Why not enjoy life now and do the things now that you are waiting to do when the time is right or when you retire? Why would you wait until the sun is setting on your life to do the things you always wanted? The answer is fear. Fear will stop you in your tracks, stranding you in that dead-end job for a mediocre paycheck. Fear is the brick wall that prevents you from living the life you want most.

You are the only obstacle that blocks the path you wish to take. YES! You are the one stopping you. Fear prevents you from taking the actions that are necessary to live life on your terms. It keeps you from becoming successful. Key notes to consider regarding fear:

We all have fear.
We all have a fear of failing.

We all have fear of rejection.
We all have fears of complacency.
We all have fears of hard work.
We all have fears of not being accepted.
We all have fears of not being smart enough.
We all have fears of being unworthy of what we
    desire.
YES, we all have fears.

All our fears, doubts, and insecurities block us from achieving what we dream of and from realizing what success really is. It traps us from living the intentional successful life we all want.

I am not perfect, and yes, I have experienced what it feels like to fail:

I have been totally broke, without enough money
    to buy gas or food for my family.
I have been unhealthy and overweight.
Several business ventures I have created failed
    miserably.
I know what it feels like to be miserable,
    depressed, and unfulfilled.
I struggle with anger management issues.
I suffer from PTSD.
I live with survivor's guilt.
I experienced a heart attack before the age of
    forty.
I was the kid in school with the high IQ making
    mediocre grades.
I passed all the physical qualifications for an elite
    military program only to be disqualified
    due to a prior injury.
I do not drink alcohol because I am unable to
    control it.
I was severely burned in a chemical plant explo-
    sion, spent time in a burn unit, and now

live with scars that act as a reminder every
day of that experience.
I know the feeling of being placed in a coma to
reduce the severe pain I was experiencing as
a result of being burned.

Yes, I know fear. I know failure and have experienced it. I know
pain and suffering. I know how all these in combination will stop
you dead in your tracks. Unfortunately, as we grow and develop from
a small child to a young adult, we develop a degree of fear. When
we are young, we take risks, we fail, we feel embarrassed, and then
learn overtime to not take risks. We justify the lack of risk-taking by
believing it is okay to be in a mediocre position at a dead-end job. It
is okay to stay in that cancerous relationship where at least you feel a
small sense of being accepted. We think, why take the risk? Why risk
taking the chance? Why not just stay in a place of comfort where we
know the chance of failure is small? It is easy to justify staying in your
comfort zone where the lemonade is icy fresh, and the breeze is cool.
But as a result of this stagnation you call comfort, you learn to hide
from the opportunities involving any type of risk. As time presses on,
you learn to never take the risk that may give you the opportunity to
be successful. In the end, you never realize your full potential because
you built an imaginary bubble to protect yourself from taking risk.
There is no need to step out and take a chance when your comfort
zone will protect you. Fear keeps you in your bubble. It may be time
for you to pop the bubble and step outside your comfort zone.

What if you take a risk that ends in failure? What if you went
against the grain? When you willingly step outside of your comfort
zone, it becomes easier to embrace your failures. As you learn to step
out of your comfort zone, you also learn how to improve and learn
from your failures. Donald Trump has stated that he has failed, COM-
PLETELY, at least eight times, but he is now one of the most successful people in the world. When the odds were against him, he was
even elected to the office of president of the United States. Why is
that? He learned from his failures. Instead of retreating, he continued
moving forward using what he learned from each of his failures. At

some point, you will start taking greater risks. With each risk you take, you will learn that you will win some and you will lose some. As you win and lose, you learn important lessons along the way from each risk you take. This cycle provides you with the tools necessary to continue taking risks you never thought you would take.

Your potential becomes unlimited when you step outside of the stagnant redundancy of your comfort zone. Once you conquer your fear by stepping out of your comfort zone, you will become a warrior with a spirit that has an unbreakable will to be whatever it is that you want to be in life. Many of us are warriors willing to step out of this zone, but there are just as many who are hypnotized by the routine of letting fear control their life. If you consider life as nothing more than a series of fights, it becomes clear that we all must fight for our dreams. We all must fight for our future. We all must fight for our children, for the new job, or the next promotion. The difficult part of this is defining who you are.

Think about how you act during your darkest moments. How do you act when life has your back against the wall? How do you handle the times when you are alone and there appears to be no tomorrow? How you deal with challenging moments will determine whether you are going to unleash your full potential or not. I want you to imagine a life where you are filled with confidence, strong work ethic, mental toughness, a warrior's spirit, complete focus, full of energy, unrelenting discipline, and a deep desire to improve. In such a life, fear will be unable to hold you back. I do not believe we were put on this earth to live an ordinary comfortable life. I believe we were put here to live our lives to the fullest potential so that we can give back more than we receive. To be able to do that, you must conquer your fears.

When it comes to success, fear is your worst enemy. When your life is controlled by fear, you will deny the risks that bring success. Great success only comes with taking greater risks. If you fear taking the greater risks, you will never achieve the greater success you desire. What many people do not understand is that the things that scare us most have the potential for the largest payoffs in our lives. I am not suggesting that the risks that scare us are easy to overcome. What I am suggesting is if you work through the fears that prevent you from taking risks, you will realize success. Great things will happen for you if you take the risk.

At some point in your life, you must decide if it is more important for you to have the courage to face your fears or cling to the comfort zone that make you feel safe. So many of our fears are irrational and make little sense. Consider this: how often do you feel afraid to make that important phone call or contact a potential client because you fear that call or meeting will not go well? "What will I do then?" you say to yourself as your trembling hands punch in the numbers on the phone. You must face the fact that you failed. For some, failing is a difficult thought to process. Irrational fears prevent you from achieving any level of success. Treat your fear as a call to action and act on what is frightening you now. Do not wait! ACT NOW! Not tomorrow. Not next week. RIGHT NOW. Call that person you need to talk with. Write that email you need to write. Say hello to that person you have wanted to talk with since you first saw them. ACT or you will forever be left behind.

Eleanor Roosevelt said, "Fear is the most devastating emotion on earth…I believe anyone can overcome fear by doing the things you fear doing, provided you keep doing them until you get a record of successful experience behind you. You gain strength, courage, and confidence by every experience in which you really stop to look fear in the face. You are able to say to yourself, 'I lived through this horror. I can take the next thing that comes along.'"

There have been several times when fear bound me to inaction, where I was willing to tolerate complacency and the feeling of being completely miserable in fear that I might lose my comfort zone. It was only after making an intentional choice to change my thinking did my life begin to change for the better. Aristotle believed courage is the most important quality in a man. He wrote, "Courage is the first of human virtues because it makes all others possible." Without courage, nothing else will be possible. In other words, if you live in fear, nothing is possible. Fear is difficult to overcome and almost impossible if you are unable to be honest with yourself about what those fears are.

I remember when I was about fourteen years old, swimming competitively was a priority. I was excited every day to go to practice to see how much faster I was able to swim. At the far end of the pool, the water became deeper as it led into the diving area. There were three diving platforms with all three at different heights: three meters, five meters, and ten meters. I remember watching and admiring the older kids dive off the five- and ten-meter platform, thinking I would love to do that someday. At my age, I could jump from these heights, but I was unable to muster the courage to try. What if I messed up and belly flopped and all the others would make fun of me? Then one day after practice, one of the older swimmers challenged me to jump off the five-meter platform. The highest I had ever tried was the three-meter diving board. I had never jumped off anything that high before, but I wasn't going to let my fears take control. I remember the fear was overwhelming as I climbed the ladder and stepped out onto the diving platform. "You won't jump! You're a chicken-shit," the older kids yelled to me as I slowly walked toward the edge. I remember freezing, stopping dead in my tracks. Time stood still. I took a deep breath, counted to three, and ran. Falling feet first, I hit the water. As I plunged to the bottom of the pool, I thought, "You're okay! You did it!" In fact, I was better than okay. The sense of overcoming my fears was a tremendous feeling. By the time I went home that night, I was jumping from the ten-meter platform. The next day, I mastered a front flip off the five-meter platform.

My sense of success transitioned into that of arrogance. I decided I would try my flip off the ten-meter platform. My calculations failed me in middescent, and as I continued to fall from the higher platform, I overrotated and landed on my back. Hitting the water on my back is comparable to hitting a brick wall. The wind was knocked out of me, and I thought for sure I was going to drown. I remember getting out of the pool, and it was weeks before I tried it again. Every day, I thought about it; and every day, my inner voice told me I was nuts, just crazy, to even think about it. Eventually, I attempted the ten-meter platform again. How many times have you tried something where you failed and it took a long time before you tried it again? For some, they never do.

Once you decide to take the risky step and jump, two obstacles are going to stand in your way: self-doubt and fear. The moment you decide you want to double your income next year, your inner voice hammers you with self-doubt. "I'll have to work twice as hard." "I won't have time for my family." "My wife is going to kill me if I have to work more hours." "I am already maxed out on time, how can I do any more than I am already doing?" "What if I get hurt and can't work?" "How will I be able to get up two hours earlier than I am already doing?" "I am too old to be thinking like this." These are all statements of self-doubt and excuses for why you should not rise to the occasion. They are excuses your mind uses to justify the reasons why it is impossible for you to achieve success. The simple thing is you know the reasons and excuses. The hard part is silencing the negative inner voices. Knowing that it is self-doubt convincing you "why not," you can confront it and silence it before it's too late. Fear, on the other hand, is a feeling. Fear of rejection, fear of failure, or fear of making a fool of yourself are all feelings. The important thing to know about these feelings is that everyone experiences them. If you overcome the feeling, you overcome the fear. Remember, there are two things that stand in your way; your self-doubt and your fear.

Why not try something different? Why not try talking to yourself like you would talk to a friend? When your friends are in a dark place, what is the first thing you do? You try to cheer them up, right? Try lifting yourself up when you feel the same way. You must reassure yourself and become your number one cheerleader, your number one fan. Start by telling yourself out loud—and yes, in the mirror—how much you have accomplished. By listing and speaking your accomplishments to yourself in the mirror, you will see that they far outweigh your failures.

One of the best practices I have found to tap into your full potential is to keep photos of your accomplishments all around you. Example: If you had a fear of flying and you took your first flight ever, post a picture of that trip in your home office, at work, or even in front of you on the dashboard of your car. The photo will remind you that you have achieved success by overcoming your fear. If you have children, of course post pictures of them. They are some of your greatest achievements. If you obtained a certification in something, post it! If you made someone smile and they sent you a thank-you note, post it where you can see it. Post it! Put it somewhere that you can see it every day.

When our brain interprets a dangerous situation, either we stand and fight, or we flee from the danger. This is known as the fight-or-flight response. We all have this as this is part of our sympathetic nervous system. What does this system have to do with our fears? When we take a good hard look at our fear, we discover our weaknesses. On many occasions, that fear is what makes us flee and settle for the flight part of the response. When you overcome your fears, you challenge your weaknesses; and by doing so, you discover your strength. You do not need to spend countless hours in therapy to identify your weaknesses. You just need to look hard within and find the answers that you know already exist. Knowledge is power, and when you act accordingly, you take the steps to leave your comfort zone and give yourself the ability to minimize your fears; you reduce your weaknesses and enhance your control.

Courage comes in many different shapes and sizes. Courage is not about getting knocked down but getting back up each time you get knocked down. Courage is the willingness to keep trying even in the face of failure. If not you, then who? If not now, then when? Your starting point is courage. Having the courage to start is the first step in achieving what you want. If you do not try, then you are guaranteed to fail. However, if you do try, it is likely the outcome will lead to success.

Courage is the understanding that you may not succeed but you are willing to keep trying until you do. If you fail the first time, it is not the end of the world. It is not even a failure. When Thomas Edison was asked about all the failures he experienced, he said, "I have not failed. I've just found 10,000 ways that won't work." Success may not show up the way you think it should, but it will show up if you keep taking steps forward. Courage is the willingness to keep taking the steps forward, trying things repeatedly until you find the right formula for your success. Courage means that you are willing to face your fear and act despite it. When you believe in yourself, when you face your fears to overcome your weaknesses and you have the courage to keep getting back up, success will be yours.

Changing How You Think Is the Difference

My youngest son competes in very tough, high-level endurance races. For two consecutive years, he competed in one of the toughest obstacle endurance races there is, the World's Toughest Mudder. At this event, I participated as his pit crew. It is a twenty-four-hour endurance race where the competitors must complete a five-mile course of very challenging obstacles. The winner is the competitor that completes the most laps on course over the span of a twenty-four-hour period. Throughout the year leading up to the race, we discussed strategies on how to be efficient so he may complete the most laps to bring home a win—NOT AN EASY TASK. During one of our strategy discussions, I told my son, "You know better than I do that the athletes who compete in these types of events are all similar in physical capabilities, so why do you think some win and others drop out long before the time limit is up?" He believes there are many reasons for it, but for me, I believe otherwise. I believe there is only one real reason why some athletes achieve success in this event and others fail. This reason is mental strength. How athletes mentally prepared themselves for the event makes the difference between accomplishing their goal and dropping out. Most of the athletes have spent months physically training and preparing for this event but have put forth little to no effort preparing mentally.

My son not only spends time training physically, but he also spends numerous hours training mentally. There is an obstacle in the race that takes a toll on many competitors, breaking them down mentally. This obstacle is like the polar plunge where the athlete slides into a pool of ice water, submerging themselves under obstacles. Even when this obstacle is not included on the race course, the chill of night takes a toll on the human body. This is bad enough during the day, but at night, you cannot see. The air temperature will be in the low forties, upper thirties, and the competitor will become exhausted and cold. Even though most of the competitors will have wet suits on, the shock of the cold temperatures will continue to mentally and physically break down the competitor's system.

To prepare for the cold temperatures that await him at these events, my son spends time in an ice bath at the gym where he trains. When he first started, he was only able to stay in the ice bath for about two minutes. Over time, he has been able to train his mind and body to acclimate to the cold temperatures and is now able to spend twenty minutes in the ice bath without a wet suit. Your conscious mind goes to battle with your goals as it tries to convince you that the water is too cold and get out now. Any time you submerge yourself into freezing water, your subconscious mind registers this feedback and sounds the alarm to your conscious mind. That alarm is the shock you experience, but if you train your mind accordingly, the tolerance to the cold will increase. Your subconscious mind stops being concerned about the shock to your system as the adaptation takes effect. As a result, the time you spend in the ice bath will increase as you endure the cold. This in turn translates to the race, allowing you to endure the freezing temperatures on course, bettering your chances of winning.

The reasons why you must train your mind are the same in business, at home, in school, in the military, and throughout your life. Your personal belief in yourself makes the difference between quitting on yourself and enduring life's challenges. The belief that you can endure the cold when you must. If you do not believe in yourself, you do not finish. As a leader, if you do not believe in your team, they will doubt themselves. If you listen to the voices in your head telling you it is too cold to go on, it is too hot to push forward, or that you are too tied down to grow in your profession, then you cannot complete the obstacle.

Many people believe the Navy SEALs and the Special Forces teams consist of these massive and physically imposing people. If you look at the training of the Special Forces, you realize that it is not as much physical training as you may think. Yes, Navy SEALs carry an inflatable boat around on a beach as a team, but it is not to build physical toughness. Rather, it is building the mental toughness that is necessary for each team member. There is no place on a SEAL team, a Special Force team, or a highly effective business team for individuals who lack the mental toughness required to achieve their objective. The ones who complete the mission or close the very tough business deals are the ones who keep going when tough situations become too difficult.

You need good thinkers on your team for many more reasons than just being mentally tough. Good thinkers solve problems that others cannot; they never lack ideas. They can mentally endure the stress of the race, the stress of the mission, and all this adds up to what is needed to succeed. They are the ones who think before responding. They are the ones who are not just telling you what you want to hear. They are not the conditioned reactive responders who respond before the question or issue is given consideration. When Adolf Hitler was rising to power, he once boosted, "What luck for rulers that men do not think." It is the one thing that truly separates successful people from unsuccessful people. If you change the way you think, you change your life.

Looking back, each time I had an advancement in my life or a big WIN in something I thought was impossible, it was only after changing the way I thought about the situation that I had a breakthrough. Anything is possible if you believe it is possible. The moment you have doubt, the moment you let doubt in, any possibilities that may have been will disappear in an instant. The moment you plant the seed of doubt, whether in yourself or someone else, it becomes a cancer that leads to a destruction of your positivity. If you plant a seed of possibility, it grows into a lifetime of accomplishments. Nothing is possible until you change your thinking to believe in your possibilities. It is not until you stop reacting and start taking time to think that possibilities will begin to arise.

Positive thinking generates revenue, it solves problems, it creates opportunities, it completes the mission or wins the race. Positive thinking will take you to the next new level in your personal and professional life. Positive thinking will change your life if you believe it will. I will be the first to tell you that changing the way you think is not a simple task. It is not an AUTOMATIC PROCESS or something you believe that will just occur on its own. It is not something you just think about and it happens. Positive thinking is something you must work on. The only people who believe thinking is easy are the ones who do not think at all. Albert Einstein reminded us about this when he said, "Thinking is hard work, that's why so few do it."

One thing to remember is that your positive thinking does not guarantee you a good life. I know many people who have had one positive thought and try to ride this idea for a lifetime only to end up unhappy with the outcome. You know who I am talking about. They are the one-hit wonders, the one-book authors, the one-message speakers, the onetime inventors. They are the ones who spend their entire life struggling to protect or promote their single idea. The truth is, success comes to those who have a mountain full of ideas they act on. Those ideas are continually mined over their lifetime and continue to build into new ideas. Success does not come to those who try to live off one idea only to result in minimal production. To become that person who can mine ideas over a lifetime, you must make time to think and brainstorm on your ideas and about the solutions for new directions. To be successful, you cannot live a life of thoughtless responses, of reacting to the market instead of being first to find the trends or living in a world of never-ending business meetings that rob you of your valuable time to think things through to consider new ideas, solutions, or directions. David Schwartz said it best when he stated, "Where success is concerned, people are not measured in inches, or pounds or college degrees, or family background; they are measured by the size of their thinking." How big is your thinking?

Your Negative Inner Voice

If you were to die today, what would you regret not being able to do? Take a moment to write down your answers.

1. Are you acting on the things you wrote down?
2. If not, why? Especially, if you would regret not being able to do them, why are you not doing them now?

What are you waiting for? If what you wrote down are that important to you, why are you not doing them? It is funny how we say one thing yet do another. Why do so many of us listen to our inner voice of doubt and fear? The same voices that we make up in our head that keep us average and mediocre. Why do you accept average and not awesome?

Our inner voice convinces us to be comfortable. The voice says, "Why try for awesome if you are doing okay at mediocracy?" As you become closer to taking the first step toward something new, the volume of your inner voices of doubt and fear will become almost deafening the closer you get. Think about what has prevented you from taking a risk. Were you listening to your inner voices of doubt and fear telling you, "Don't do it. Why are you doing this?" The problem with this is that it is your own self, your own inner voices that are telling you that you are not good enough to take the necessary steps. Your inner voices are telling you things without even knowing the facts as though they have become the absolute authority. Those inner voices of doubt and fear that you hear are made up by you in your mind. Your inner voices of doubt and fear provide the excuses you need to avoid difficult situations or making tough decisions.

How many times have you heard, "Trust your inner voice" or "What's your inner voice telling you?" Time and again, my inner voices were key in helping me achieve. The difference is I do not let my inner voice of doubt and fear have a say on my actions. By shutting down my doubt and fear, I control my own life. Over the years, I have spoken with many people regarding business. I have started a few small businesses with a few failures and a few successes. Many of the individuals I have spoken to expressed their unhappiness with where they were in their career or life. I would ask, "Have you ever thought about starting your own business?" or "Why not find another job or career that makes you happy?" The common response I receive is, "Oh, I can't do that" or "I could never start a business" or "I am not trained for…" With each response, I follow with, "Why can't you? Have you already considered it?" My questions always open the floodgates of excuses, almost always ending with, "I just know inside it's not right for me."

When you stop accepting the average path and learn to embrace the difficult challenges life brings, you become engaged with the world around you and learn how to silence the inner voice of fear and doubt. If left unchecked, your inner voices will become self-deprecating and will chisel away at your confidence, self-esteem, and self-worth. If allowed to happen long enough, they will become habits that become ingrained in your comfort zone. If allowed to persist, no matter what people say to help build you up, your inner voices will not be silenced. Consider this from authors David Molden and Pat Hutchinson:

> *We all have a tendency to judge, speculate and compare, as your inner voice describes what you see and hear in terms of good/bad, right/wrong, small/ large, perfect/imperfect, must/mustn't, can/can't, should/shouldn't, etc. If this type of thinking leaves you feeling anxious, angry or sad, your self-confidence will take a knocking. Whilst most people make judgments, confident people do so the least; they are more inclined to be curious about the world and seek to understand it, not judge it. When you understand, you can be confident.*
>
> *Confident people often have a code for how they engage with the world, like a set of principles to live by, such as "trust what people do, not what they say they will do," or "help other people along the way whenever you can." This is what their inner voices used for—to keep life-principles at the forefront of their mind. This helps them make quick decisions and feel certain about themselves.*

Stop shooting yourself in the foot by allowing your negative thoughts run your life. Start today by listening to what you are saying to yourself and silence the negative voices that prevent you from growing. Ask yourself a simple question, "Is my thought helpful or hurtful to me?"

Think Big

When you think about where you want to be next year or in years to come, do you aim for the stars? Do you envision goals for yourself that are so large that many people believe they are not achievable? Or do you set safe, comfortable small goals that are easy to achieve? When you set your sights on something big, it opens your world to significant opportunities. When you think big and set extraordinary goals that you may not reach, there is a chance you will become close to what you set out to achieve. When you think big and set risky goals, you do not place limitations on the results as you do when thinking small and creating easy to achieve goals.

A common trait shared by successful people is the ability to think big and set extraordinary goals. The problem is most people have been conditioned to abide to a certain comfortable mind-set. Thinking outside of that conditioned comfortable mind-set is too risky for them to comprehend. Thinking big and setting large goals challenges the limiting mind-set. Consider the Wright brothers. The mind-set during their time was that humans were unable to fly. If the Wright brothers had not challenged the idea of why humans are unable to fly, where would we be today? What if Bill Gates did not challenge the conventional wisdom that great business success is only achieved through a Harvard education? He dreamed big, dropped out of college, and started Microsoft.

Thinking big will challenge you to go beyond your comfort zone and will push you beyond what you believe are your only options. Donald Trump believes that "most people think small because most people are afraid of success, afraid of making decisions, afraid of winning. And that gives people like me a great advantage." It is easy to focus on shortcomings and failures, making it difficult to see the clear path to achieving big goals. However, setting substantial goals challenges you to expand beyond your means rather than existing at or below what you have grown accustomed to. People who live below their full potential are those who are small thinkers and average achievers. People like Donald Trump, Bill Gates, and Steve Jobs do not live below their means. They grow and act on the full potential achieving their desired lifestyle. Extraordinary thinkers do not accept average results; they strive for excellence.

When you think big, you provide yourself with a sense of purpose. It provides you with something worth pursuing. President Kennedy was a big thinker. When he set the goal to put a man on the moon, it became a nation's challenge that was worth pursuing and, in the end, provided purpose for many individuals. The Wright brothers' notion of human flight became their life's purpose. We all have a purpose here on earth. The challenge becomes thinking big enough to discover yours.

When you picture yourself realizing success, how do you imagine it looking? Are you the type of person that bets on the lottery for achieving success, or are you setting your sights on real achievements by acquiring the building blocks necessary to construct your own success? Are you counting on yourself and working toward your own goals that you set, or are you counting on others and working toward what they want to achieve? Howard Hughes once said, "I intend to be the richest man in the world." Are you a Howard Hughes–type person, or are you giving others the advantage by being just average?

Mental Toughness

Life Will Be Challenging

*Life can be a challenge, life can seem impossible, but
it's never easy when there's so much on the line.*
                                                    —Herman Cain

Life is challenging, full of choices and decisions that need to be made. Every day, these choices and decisions present themselves as challenges. How we handle these challenges and compose ourselves will define who we are. As challenging as life can be, what would life be without challenges? Life has taught me there are two types of people. Those who are willing to do whatever it takes to make a difference in their life and those who are paralyzed by the fear of failure who do not take the chance. What type of person are you?

They say life happens, and with it comes challenges in all shapes and sizes. Daily, we face the challenges that shape our life path, and then there are the challenges that shape our entire course. Life has a way of presenting us with new and unexpected challenges that will block our path and force us to adjust. These challenges can be the most difficult to overcome but can also be the most rewarding. Regardless of the challenge at hand, they help build our character, strengthen us mentally, and teach the lessons that are necessary to survive.

Throughout my journey, I have overcome many difficult and challenging situations that have molded my character into the person I am today. From terrorist attacks, to surviving a chemical plant explosion, to fears of losing a child to war, to receiving the phone call that my daughter and her family have been in a terrible automobile accident, to the realization that the day has come where your children are all grown and the house is empty.

My wife and I had been looking forward to the day we would have our lives back. No more running to this baseball practice and that soccer practice. No more school meetings or private school tuition. No more Friday nights at the football field followed by dinner in the local diner. No more pestering about homework, which always became our problem. We thought life would be amazing when the nest became empty. I remember telling my wife how much fun we were going to have. How much of our life we would be getting back.

I remember vividly our youngest son's last high school football game. It was a state playoff game, and his team had just lost. I remember how I felt. The thoughts of grief were strong as the tears started to fill my eyes. I would learn quickly that I would miss it all. I remember the sense of pride my wife and I felt when our son received a scholarship to play college football. The stage was set for him to be the first person in the family to play college football. I will never forget the feeling I felt the day we pulled away from the dorm. I remember thinking my life as I have known it to this point: will never again be the same.

What is interesting is the idea that we have been preparing him for this event. Long strenuous days of practice and camps sped by without giving it a second thought that my wife and I needed to prepare ourselves for the day our youngest child would leave the nest. Even though we knew it was coming, it blindsided us, and it took time to come to terms with our new life.

The ending to a chapter is not all that bad. Unbeknownst to me, I had gone through a life challenge that helped write a new chapter in my life. I worked through that lost feeling I had from no longer being at the field or in the field house. This challenge proved to me that there is life after football. A sense of stability returned to my life as I met the challenge head-on as I moved into this new chapter of my life.

What I have learned from dealing with life challenges is that much of what makes a challenge seem insurmountable is caused by our perspective. Do you see the glass half full or half empty? Instead of focusing on how bad and unfair a life challenge is, focus on the possibility of how good things will be when you overcome the inconvenient situation that is presented to you. With a positive attitude, you are already halfway to overcoming any challenge. Most importantly, what I have learned is that life is a series of calmness, periods of confusion, change, and then transition, which brings you back to a new beginning. Knowing this has made the thought of accepting and facing the next challenge that much easier.

At some point in our lives, we will all face tough challenges that are difficult to overcome, especially when your back is against the wall and the odds are stacked against you. Certainly, many challenges will be hard. Certainly, many will be life changing. And certainly, if you do not try to overcome, you will never know what might have been. Back in 1990, a close childhood friend told me prior to leaving for the first Persian Gulf War in Iraq something I will never forget. I remember him telling me that the both of us could achieve anything by just remembering to never give in, never give up, and never surrender. Those eight words, "never give in, never give up, never surrender," have been embedded in my memory ever since. To face life challenges and win, you must have those eight words engraved within your own purpose. With those eight words, you can overcome anything you set your mind to.

Throughout our journey in life, we will come to many crossroads. We will be faced with many challenges, with many obstacles, and make terrible choices. It is what you do after making these bad choices that will define you and give you the biggest potential to change your life. In the words of Martin Luther King Jr., "The true measure of a man is not how he behaves in moments of comfort and convenience but how he stands at times of controversy and challenges."

For many, it is easy to play the role of the victim, to blame others, to even blame fate when unplanned life challenges show up in their life. As a result, we fail to realize that those unplanned trials and tribulations are extraordinary opportunities that test how willing we are to live up to the pursuit of our dreams. How willing are you to take full responsibility for your own choices and outcomes? How willing are you to plow up your life to reveal what weaknesses you have? Are you prepared to do whatever it takes to make a breakthrough? Abraham Lincoln had two failed businesses, one nervous breakdown, endured the death of his sweetheart, and was defeated for public office more than ten times. Life will be challenging.

No one wants to experience adversity, but we all will. The way you choose to act when faced with adversity will have a great impact on your life. If you fear failure and choose not to take the risk necessary to move forward, then the fear of failure will rule your life. Challenges come in all shapes and sizes. There are "the comfort zone" challenges. "The fear that you cannot rise to the occasion" challenges. "The fatigue of trying to get something off the ground" challenges. Regardless of the type of challenge, each will impact your life differently.

Life challenges will test you your entire life. You lose your job, you are challenged to find another one. You qualify for a home loan, you must rise to the challenge of paying the mortgage for the next fifteen or thirty years. It is important to remember that whatever challenges you face, you are being equipped to become a better you, a stronger, more resilient YOU—the type of person that can achieve more and climb to greater heights than you ever envisioned for yourself.

Hard Work Is a Turning Point

Have you passed up chances to try something new because you were nervous about whether you can do it or feared what others might say? Maybe it is time for you to start creating your own opportunities at work and in your personal life. Have you thought about the steps needed to make what you want a reality? Anything worth having will take hard work and dedication to get. Maybe it is hard work you are afraid of. How bad do you want whatever it is that you want? Are you willing to roll up your sleeves and put in the hard work?

Your turning point is the moment you take that first step toward an opportunity that will change your life. That first step takes effort and courage. It is not so much a physically hard step as it is a mentally demanding leap you must take. Hard work does pay off in many ways. One of the most important aspects I have learned regarding hard work is that it cannot be faked. Hard work is necessary in everything you do. It cannot be circumvented, skipped, or artificially accelerated. You must put in the effort and be dedicated to what needs to be done. This is the very essence of hard work.

If I apply myself and work hard, I could achieve anything. This is a lesson that was instilled in me many years ago by my mentors. I have come to accept this lesson as a life truth, and over the years, I have shared this with anyone who would listen. The downfall of this truth is the feeling that we are working hard but it just seems like we are never getting anywhere. This false feeling is untrue! The simple act of starting the process of going after what you want moves you down the path toward achievement. It moves you off the starting blocks and one step closer to the end goal. Don't let the hardest thing you ever do be the act of getting started. JUST GET STARTED!

Motivation

Only I can change my life. No one can do it for me.
—Carol Burnett

Over the years, I have heard many individuals say, "Well, what's your motivation?" "What motivates you to do what you do?" "Aren't you motivated?" "Where's your motivation?" "You lack motivation." We have all heard it time and again. Many of us have asked those questions of someone, and I am quite sure many of you have been asked about your own motivations.

Recently, I saw a young lady on a talk show saying motivation does not exist. She believes motivation is something that is made up. That no one can motivate you to do anything, not even yourself. Obviously, this person has never been challenged in a way that places her in a scenario where she was forced to face a life-or-death situation. Believe me, when you are placed in a dangerous situation, the motivation to survive becomes apparent. I believe you can look at it in two ways: you motivate yourself to get yourself out of whatever the situation is, or the situation itself becomes the motivation needed to stay and fight.

For many, their motivation has been the idea of a successful outcome, a win. I like to say, "WINNING!" Motivation is what keeps you moving toward the prize, the achievement, the success you seek. Something I have used is visualizing myself reaching that prize, that goal, that success I wanted. That vision of success will keep you focused on what it takes to get you there.

Another statement that has kept me going when I needed motivation is, "You can't beat me," or "This can't beat me." When my children played youth sports, high school varsity sports, and college sports, they would say self-discouraging statements as they second-guessed their abilities. Statements like "I don't know, Pops, this is hard" or "I'm not good enough" were often heard when challenging times occurred on the field. I would always remind them, "Yes, you are good enough, and you can't be beat." When my youngest played college football, he adopted this phrase: "You can't beat me." On the field, he was often heard yelling this statement to the opposing players. It was his motivation to win and to succeed. "You can't beat me." "I will outwork you." "I will outplay you." What this short saying did was to focus each one of them on what mattered most, staying focused or motivated on the result. To succeed.

Ask yourself, "Why do I want this so badly? Why is it important to achieve this goal?" When thinking of these two questions and the saying "You can't beat me," it becomes rather clear how this all works together. Why do I want to so badly? I do not like to be beat. Why is it important to achieve this goal? I do not like to be beat. When you figure out the answers to these questions, you will understand your motivation and desires. When you understand your motivations, it becomes much easier to clearly define your objectives: what it is you want and why.

My son recently created a blog called Mile 12 Concept, which can be found at www.mile12concept.com. On this site, there is a post titled "What Is Mile 12 Concept?" Take a moment and read this post. The writer, who is also my youngest son, explains how in many ways motivation is really nothing more than an idea or vision. The post talks about how, in the middle of the night soaking wet, cold to the bone, halfway through a twenty-four-hour race, he questions his reasons for being there. He searches for the meaning of his why. Through self-conflict and doubt, he pushes on through the night, discovering why it was important to do what he was doing. At that moment on the course, climbing a mountain in the pitch-black dead of night wearing nothing but a wet suit and a head lamp, he realized what his true motivation was. You will have to read it to find out.

Confidence

No one can make you feel inferior without your consent.
—*Eleanor Roosevelt*

On a scale of 1 to 10, where do you score your confidence? For some, understanding confidence can be very difficult especially when trying to link it with mental toughness. Confidence plays a vital role in developing mental toughness. *Merriam-Webster*'s dictionary defines *confidence* as

1. "a feeling or consciousness of one's powers or of reliance on one's circumstances,"
2. "faith or belief that one will act in a right, proper, or effective way," and
3. "the quality or state of being certain."

I define *confidence* as my personal belief that I have what it takes to overcome any obstacles that are on my way as I go after my goals. You may win, and you may lose. But the important thing to remember is that you have the confidence to at least try. What I have learned about confidence is that when it is high, you are able to bounce back from failures, mistakes, and poor performance much quicker than those who are lacking it.

Highly successful people have a high level of confidence in their ability to win and achieve. But they are not born this way. They earn it, slowly developing it through time and learning through each experience. They gain their confidence through repeatedly putting themselves in the game, taking the risks, and learning from their failures and successes. Overtime, knowing that you have previously endured difficult situations, you take the time to study and learn from those past experiences. This leads to a growth in confidence as you attack business deals, sports, relationships, education, and life. An important aspect of confidence to remember is that it is an essential quality for succeeding and the recipe for building mental toughness. I believe it is one of the most critical traits and is essential for setting high goals and persevering to achieve them.

Another crucial aspect about confidence that I have learned is how contagious it can become. Like-minded people stick together, and the saying "Birds of a feather flock together" is true. Whether it's in business, coaching sports, or spending time in the military, confident people tend to associate both personally and professionally with others who have the same degree of confidence. I am a firm believer that "you become who you associate with." I have observed individuals with low levels of confidence be assigned to teams that have an abundance of confident team members transformed into confident individuals. Your confidence shines in the way you carry yourself. Most times, it is the determining factor in whether you win or lose. When you confidently demonstrate self-control over your emotions, your actions, and the situation, others take notice. They recognize you as a leader that they are willing to trust and follow.

On the other side of the spectrum, individuals with low confidence continuously complain about everything while showing off to gain attention and recognition. Many times, they will turn to destructive habits such as substance abuse. Their lack of confidence shines bright as they are on the constant hunt for praise and approval. Their projections of self-pity shine and become clear as they try to draw you in closer so you may go down with their ship. Once you allow the thought of quitting into your mind, you are on a direct path to failing. When you feel sorry for yourself, you begin the process of sinking and destroying your confidence as the guarantee of your own demise becomes evident.

Your confidence is the result of your life experiences and actions. Your confidence can be increased, but it takes work. Confidence can be developed through time whether it's a few weeks, a few months or even a few years. Although you can develop your confidence, there is no guarantee that it will improve. There is no set formula, but if you work hard at the following three points, you might be surprised:

1. Set personal and professional goals. Everyone needs a starting point and a target. Most importantly, you simply need to decide if it is time to get started.
2. Prepare yourself. Once you know what your starting point is and what target you placed in your crosshairs, you need to diligently plan your course. What will it take? I have found that by discovering what it takes to achieve the goal, your confidence will elevate.
3. Visualize your success. Your success depends on your ability to visualize it. If you cannot visualize yourself succeeding, you fail. But if you can see yourself achieving, then anything is possible.

You can directly manipulate your level of confidence; all you need to do is believe it.

Focus

Always focus on the front windshield and not the review mirror.
—Colin Powell

Growing up, I was often reminded to keep my eyes on the prize. I heard it from my parents, my scoutmaster, coaches, while in the military, and in business. It was not until much later in life did I fully understand how important this simple phrase was to my success. As I matured and began to pay closer attention to successful people, I

171

realized that they maintain an unrelenting focus on what matters in life regardless of the distractions around them. Successful people focus on their accomplishments rather than their failures. They are keenly engaged and focus on the next steps needed for their goals rather than wasting valuable time on the distractions around them. Successful people have an ability to consistently be proactive in their pursuit of success.

Focus is your ability to stay engaged without distraction toward an objective. On a scale of 1 to 10, where do you rank your ability to remain focused? Focus is necessary if you want to develop mental toughness that enables you to achieve your goals. It is a trait you must master if you want to stay on track when undertaking any challenge.

When developing your mental toughness, your ability to establish effective personal habits such as focus is vital. One way to improve your ability to focus is by establishing small goals so you are achieving victories toward the greater accomplishment you are seeking. When I made the decision to lose weight, I did not start out by deciding I was going to lose sixty-eight pounds in six months. I set my focus on losing a pound or two a day. I did not set out vowing I would eat right for the next six months; rather, I set my target on eating correctly and establishing an exercise routine that I could adhere to. By doing this, I was able to focus on small victories for the greater accomplishment. I did not let myself become distracted by what seemed an impossible task over an impossible amount of time. I realized at the end of the first day that if I could focus on doing what I needed to do that first day, I could do it again the next day. I created new eating habits, and I was motivated at beating myself each day. If you can do it the first day, you can do it even better the second day, and the third day and so on.

An individual that I coached with once asked, "How do you eat an elephant?" At that time, I told him I had no idea. He laughed and told me, "You eat an elephant one bite at a time!" In other words, to succeed, all you really need to do is focus on the task at hand. Nothing else. Over time, you will succeed. To win those small victories, establish a daily schedule for yourself that includes specific actions in a measurable way. Once you develop your routine, become obsessed with it and work toward winning small victories every day. When you focus on your behavior, the results will follow.

Staying focused:

Find—identify what you need to improve on to be successful.

Organize—organize and establish an action plan that helps you improve upon what you identified above.

Collect—research and collect data you need to move forward with your action plan.

Understand—understand all the variables and potential risks involved in making your improvements.

Start—execute your action plan. The only way you focus is to start.

Composure

The beauty of the soul shines out when a man bears with composure one heavy mischance after another, not because he does not feel them, but because he is a man of high and heroic temper.

—Aristotle

They say when the going gets tough, the tough get going. Do you? Are you tough enough to get going when the going gets tough? Your composure is your ability to remain calm and in control when demanding situations present themselves. Your composure in difficult situations will be the difference in whether you win or lose or, for some, living or dying. Composure can be defined as your ability to stay in control of yourself in a manner that allows you to continue to perform at optimum levels regardless of the situation. As we grow and learn through our experiences, we learn how to respond in certain situations. Your brain and mind are two separate entities. The body obeys the brain, and the brain obeys the mind. As a result, there are certain emotions and reactions your brain automatically produces in response to specific situations. Knowing how all this works and what responses will occur during each situation gives you an advantage. This advantage enables you to act properly with expected responses by overriding your brain's response. This allows you to control your own actions without reflex.

Composure enables you to have clarity of your thoughts and the ability to maintain your focus during stressful situations. Your brain will tell you that you are too cold, too hot, too tired, too weak, too wet, too old, or you just do not have what it takes. Individuals who listen to these unwarranted stimuli are the ones who lose their composure and focus, eventually giving up on themselves. However, those who maintain their composure are just the opposite; they maintain their focus on the task while committing to doing their very best to succeed. By remaining composed, they can dig deep within themselves to find the inner strength they need to finish.

Countless times in my life, my brain has told me that I was unable to go on, but my mind continued to push me to not stop. At some point, we all experience situations in which our brain tells us we cannot go any farther, but our mind convinces us to keep going. In those situations, we must ensure our mind remains in control, providing us with the composure required to continue until we have overcome the challenge.

When we can train our mind in a way that allows us to remain composed, regardless of the situation, we ensure our ability to maintain our self-control. To a large degree, our ability to succeed depends on a mind that is conditioned to handle a difficult situation in a composed, self-controlled, manner. If you can maintain composure, it becomes easier to identify situations that trigger your brain's response mechanisms that directly impact your ability to perform at a higher level. By recognizing this pattern, you are better prepared to handle the challenging situation at hand.

There are many examples of how composure has defined past leaders, great athletes, and scholars. Lincoln is a great example. During his most trying hours, he remained patient, poised, and maintained his self-control, which history shows made all the difference.

If you fail to maintain your composure, you are not only likely to injure others, but it is certain you will injure yourself. The easiest way to remain composed in challenging situations is to remember the three keys to composure.

Composure CT3:

Control your **Thoughts**
Control your **Temper**
Control your **Tongue**

When you control your **composure CT3**, you win without regret.

Resilience

The greatest glory in living lies not in never
failing, but in rising every time we fail.
—Nelson Mandela

How quick are you to give up? When the going gets tough, are you willing to give up or give in? Your resilience is your unwillingness to give up; *"never give in, never give up, never surrender."* An important note about this saying is that even after I served in the military many years ago, it remains relevant in my life today. It is a creed I continue to live by daily. Although you will experience challenging times, many of the challenges you will face in life are not life-or-death situations. Many of the situations you experience are very difficult at best, and many can be life-changing with profound effects on who we are.

Resilience and your persistence to succeed is about having the ability to face difficult challenges, bounce back from failures, and continue to move forward toward your goals. Those who are successful in life and accomplish challenging goals are those who are willing to keep pushing forward through the heartache, hardships, pain, and self-doubt until they succeed. They are simply willing to never give in, never give up, and never surrender.

There is a Special Forces instructor that tells a story about candidates reporting to training. Before a required forced march with full gear, candidates often explained to him their previous accomplishments such as triathlons, marathons, or that they have black belts in martial arts. When the candidates were done predicting where they would finish amongst the ranks, the instructor would simply reply, "That's impressive. We'll have to find out if you can do it when your socks are wet."

After looking at thirty years of results from the program, the instructor found that 50 percent of the candidates dropped out after the forced march. This march included an overnight hike through the wetlands where the candidate's socks became soaked with muck. In the end, people quit because they refused to go on due to the pain and discomfort from marching in wet socks. In other words, it does not matter what your prior experiences are, your achievements, your physical conditioning, or your level of endurance; rather, what matters is the mental capacity and willingness to persist in difficult circumstances while maintaining a level of resilience to push through the challenge.

In my life, I have learned that most people stop working at the first sign of fatigue or difficult challenge. They simply quit and walk away. However, an unusual thing happens when they decide to keep pushing forward even when they are exhausted. People can move past the fatigue and exhaustion to gain a second, third, or even fourth wind that provides them the energy to continue. Individuals who are resilient utilize their deepest energy stores that they can call up on demand. The ability to call on this energy is where many of us fail.

Only very few individuals ever make serious demands of themselves. We see this across all aspects of life. Many of us miss succeeding at the greater accomplishments because we give up too soon. We raise the white flag and surrender at the first signs of anything hard or challenging.

Resilience is the glue that binds motivation, confidence, focus, and composure together, providing you undeniable mental toughness. If you are unwilling to bounce back after a failure, it does not matter how developed your other mental toughness traits are. In the end, you still fail.

Mental toughness is a choice we make to quit or keep going. A famous quote from the late Vince Lombardi that I find to have significant value and is a constant reminder to me to keep moving forward is, "It's not whether you get knocked down, it's whether you get up." Instead of letting setbacks and failures dominate their reality, resilient people find a way to continue through hardships.

Four key points to building an undeniable resilience:

- **Have a positive attitude**—a positive attitude pushes you toward the finish. A negative attitude kills you at the start.
- **Be optimistic**—the glass is half full not half empty.
- **Control your emotions**—responding to a difficult challenge with negative emotions will lead to failure. Create a positive outlook and emotion that will lead you to the success you seek.
- **Embrace your failures and see them as an opportunity to learn**—view your failures as a means for gathering feedback regarding the situation rather than a defeat.

Even after the most significant of misfortunes, resilient people are willing to change course and continue to move toward, achieving the result they desire.

Wrapping Up Mental Toughness

Since my first radio show regarding mental toughness, I have received many emails and phone calls from people willing to debate what traits really make up mental toughness. Many of those who contacted me believe there are more traits and not just the five I have listed. Others believe that each trait individually will provide a mentally tough mind. That all five traits are not necessary. I appreciate the discussion, and everyone is entitled to their opinion, but I stand my ground on my belief that all five traits are needed: motivation, confidence, focus, composure, and resilience. If you take a moment to consider this perspective, you will begin to realize that several traits cannot be mastered without developing several of the other traits. For example, if you are confident but lack motivation, you will never start what you want to accomplish. If you are both motivated and confident but lack focus, you will become distracted from the task and unable to see it to completion. If you have all the traits except for composure, you will never accomplish the task when the pressure of possible failure arises.

Some people have challenged my assertion that setting goals requires a degree of mental toughness. Following a presentation, I gave an individual said to me, "You must be able to set goals and follow through with them, but not giving 100 percent or not having the five traits you mentioned doesn't always lead to failure." After considering his statement I replied, "Yes, but how do you do that if you are not motivated? What if you lack enough confidence to create the goals? How do you stay on task to complete the goals if you cannot focus? How do you finish if you blow up every time you hit a roadblock? How do you see your goals through to completion if you lack resilience or enough staying power to finish?"

Others have told me, "You need to be driven, willing to work hard and make sacrifices." I follow up with a simple question, "How do you do that without mental toughness?"

The key to understanding mental toughness is the essential quality that is critical to your ability to successfully achieve your goals regardless of what those goals are. The greater the level of difficulty or risk needed to achieve your goals, the more important your mental toughness becomes.

Mental toughness is that inner spark and inner strength that comes from deep inside of you. It ignites the fire of your conscious and rational thought in your brain that allows you to decide if you have had enough and it is time to give up. Once your brain has resigned itself to give in, the only will that allows you to push forward is energized by the power you have deep within that is generated through your mental toughness. When this power takes control in a mentally tough individual, it engulfs their entire being and stays with them until they emerge triumphant.

The problem is, this does not work for many people because they are lacking in one or more of the five mental toughness traits. Think about the last time you gave in or gave up on a goal. What was the reason you quit? The many answers I receive for these questions are excuses that include the lack of money, lack of skills, lack of time, or unsuccessful in gaining traction on achieving the goal.

When you say you lack money, you are saying you lack motivation to generate money and do not have the confidence in your abilities to earn it. When you say you do not have the time or you are not moving fast enough toward achieving your goal, what I hear is a lack in resilience. Can you see how this all works? If you are motivated and have confidence in your abilities, you can learn any skill needed to achieve a desired goal.

Every year, an annual congressional baseball game is held between members of congress. In 2017, this game became a much different event. Prior to the game, a gunman opened fire at one of the practices and shot several of those participating, one of which was the congressional house whip. Every account of what happened credits the two special agents assigned to protect the house whip with saving the lives of those there. The agents could have easily run for cover with the rest and wait for backup, but they did not. They confronted the shooter head-on, and a gun battle ensued. If it was not for the mental toughness of these agents, it is very possible many lives could have been lost. The service agent's training promotes their abilities to protect the individuals they are assigned to. These abilities are based on the sound fundamentals of mental toughness. They must be motivated and confident in their skills to protect those they are assigned to at all cost. They must be able to focus and maintain composure on what is important when trouble arises. Their composure ensures that they remain calm, cool, and collected in the heat of battle. Their resilience toward protecting each individual is key as it can be the difference between life and death for the person they are assigned to.

Extensive training and preparation are the keys to your mental toughness. You can't just wake up one morning and declare that you are now mentally tough. You must continually work to develop the five traits: motivation, confidence, focus, composure, and resilience. It takes time, action, and continuous work. One of the easiest things you can do to start building your mental toughness is to simply decide to start. Once you decide, action is required. Even the smallest step toward a goal is a step closer to achieving that goal. The longer you wait to take that first step, the longer it will take to achieve what you desire. Once you decide to act, you will find that every step you take thereafter will become easier to make. As you take each step, you will become more motivated, more confident, more focused, more composed, and more resilient.

The most important thing to remember from all this is that you must take the first step to begin your journey toward your definition of success. The best way to achieve the success you want is to simply begin. If you are unwilling to change, you will not see the change around you. Mental toughness is a choice. A choice whether to continue or to quit. Nothing more.

Your Next Steps

All Things Are Possible

Pain is temporary—however, if I quit it will last forever.
—Ray Lewis

There are times when life knocks you down and you feel like you have no strength left to continue. Those are the times that will define who you are. It is when your inner voice tells you, "It's possible, just get back up and keep going." All things are possible, but you must be willing to push yourself. That first act is the most important, and you must have faith, courage, and confidence in yourself. It does not matter what others think or believe about you. What matters most is how you think and believe in yourself.

There is great potential within you. Everyone has it, but not everyone believes it. Listen to yourself when your inner voice says, "This is what I believe, and I am willing to do anything for it." We are all made to shine, not just some of us. The problem is not everyone believes they can shine as bright as others, or for that matter, shine at all. If you do not believe in yourself, who will?

Do you want more from life? Or is being average where you want to be? If you had one shot at what you really wanted, would you take it? Or would you let it slip away, fearing you might fail? The question becomes how bad do you really want your one shot—bad enough to do whatever it takes to achieve it? If not, have you considered what you will do with the rest of your life? Of course, you can survive on mediocrity, but is that living?

The most important and most successful parts of your life may still be in front of you. Inside each of us, there is untapped potential waiting for you to act upon it. What you decide to do with this untapped potential is the difference between success, failure, or mediocrity. An individual's potential for success is unlimited so long as they choose to keep moving toward it. You must be willing to look past the obstacles with a larger view of the world.

Do you have the confidence to seize the opportunities ahead of you? You and only you are the one that makes the decision on which path to take. Only you make the choice to not let others stand in your way. Believing in yourself and your unlimited potential makes the impossible possible. When you believe in yourself, anything is possible.

Let go of the baggage that is holding you back. Look past the obstacles that blind you from what is achievable. Most importantly, decide to succeed no matter what it takes. Dream big, succeed big. Henry Ford said, "Whether you think you can or you think you can't, you're right." If you want something bad enough, then go after it and do not stop until you get it. Things do not always work out the way we would like. However, if you do not try, you will never know the outcome of what could have been. When you do not give up, you do not fail, so never give up in your pursuit of success.

Nothing Is Guaranteed

When I think about life and the many choices I have made, it reminds me of the many roads I have ventured down over the course of my journey. In my life, I have been on many different roads, even passed up driving on some of the roads that just seemed too risky. There are long roads and short roads. Some are smooth and others are rocky. There are winding roads and straight roads. There are roads that will play you a tune if you drive just right on them. Just as driving on the many different roads we come across, we also come across many different life roads we end up taking. Some roads lead to fame and fortune, others to poverty and despair.

Just like the highways of the world, our roads through life have detours, red lights, corners, crossroads, and four-way stops. Taking any one of the many paths requires making choices. Many of us come to crossroads without a map and have no idea which path to take. How do you know which road is the right road? How do you know the one you take is the right road for you? Or are you stranded at the crossroad unable to take any road? The life roads we take define our lives and who we are. Not taking any road at a crossroad also defines who we are and what our life will become.

This reminds me of a Robert Frost poem. Its relevance is just as strong today as it was when I first read his words when I was much younger.

"The Road Not Taken"

Two roads diverged in a yellow wood,
And sorry I could not travel both
And be one traveler, long I stood
And looked down one as far as I could
To where it bent in the undergrowth;

Then took the other, as just as fair,
And having perhaps the better claim,
Because it was grassy and wanted wear;
Though as for that the passing there
Had worn them really about the same,

And both that morning equally lay
In leaves no step had trodden black.
Oh, I kept the first for another day!
Yet knowing how way leads on to way,
I doubted if I should ever come back.

I shall be telling this with a sigh
Somewhere ages and ages hence:
Two roads diverged in a wood, and I—

I took the one less traveled by,
And that has made all the difference.

In so many ways, this poem has made all the difference in my
life. Whenever I come to crossroads in my life, my inner voice reminds
me to "take the road less traveled, it will make all the difference."

What I find most interesting about life is that we are only guaranteed one thing: at some point, we will die. Some have argued that
we are also guaranteed birth; however, with recent bills being signed
into law, even childbirth is not guaranteed. If we are fortunate enough
to make it to birth, the countdown to your last breath begins.

One of the most important life lessons I have learned is that
there are no guarantees in life. When you think about the idea of no
guarantees except for the end life, it can be difficult to make a choice
on what life path you want to take. Regardless which path you decide
to take, you really have no idea where it will lead to until you take
it. There are no guarantees on the journey, only the results. As so
many people believe, there is no guarantee that choosing to do the
right thing will always lead to happiness. If you love someone with all
your heart, there is no guarantee that love will be reciprocated. Many
people believe by gaining fame and fortune, winning the lottery, or
having all the money you need will guarantee happiness. It does not.
The only thing you have power over are the choices you make and
how you react to consequences of your choices. Regardless of the
choices you make, there are no guarantees the choices will produce
the outcomes you expect.

There is always a guaranteed consequence to your choice.
Whether the results are good or bad, it is guaranteed the choices
you make will have consequences. Then why decide if you know the
choice is wrong and the consequences are guaranteed? Why decide
if you know from the beginning that it is not the right decision to
make? This is where people become stranded at a crossroad on their
journey. Their mind convinces them it is not the right decision, so
they take the safe, already-traveled route. You must make choices,
and only after you reflect on the choice made will you know if they

were right or wrong. If the outcomes are successful, then you made the right choice. Otherwise, your choice was wrong.

Your entire life is nothing more than a series of choices. Think about your day, everything you do is based on a choice. Some choices are subconsciously chosen: do I turn right or left, do I have a cheese sandwich or peanut butter and jelly? Other choices are more complex and have a level of risk. If there are no guarantees and you'll never know if a choice was right or wrong unless the choice is made, then you might as well take the risk. Yes, by using this approach, I have taken the wrong roads in life. There have been many situations where I have made the wrong turn and became totally lost. I have also made the right decisions that opened doors to new opportunities that I would have not had if I had failed to make a choice. In other words, I have been a lost life traveler, and I have also been an accidental tourist. Do not be fooled; the choices you make cannot be made haphazardly.

Taking risks and making choices does not mean you have the right to act carelessly. You must know your Ws—*who, what, when, where, and why.* What's involved? Who's involved? When will it happen? Where will it lead me? Why should I be involved? Asking questions is an ideal place to start when making choices or decisions. Many times, people are indecisive because they lack the necessary information that is required when making a choice. Failing to ask for information and research will lead to the inability to choose and, ultimately, failure. You need to weigh your options, understand the possible outcomes, and do not discount anything. I have found that many times the most outrageous option has proven to be the right one. There are people who create a list of pros and cons about the decisions they need to make. Using a pros and cons list provides insight on the possible consequences.

You must trust yourself. You must have confidence, considering there are no guarantees. No one is perfect, and from time to time, we make bad choices. You will never know until you accept the risk and make the choice of what you chose was right. Make a choice then believe that you are choosing the best option at that point. Once you make your choice, be ready to face its consequences. Good or bad, you own the results.

The decisions you make may take you to great success or knock you down to a bottomless pit. Regardless, whether the results were good or bad, you made a choice to live your life instead being a passive observer to your own life. Whatever the outcome of your choices is, never regret the choices you make. Instead, learn from them. Until you reach that one certainty that we are all guaranteed, you will always have the chance to make better choices. So, take the risk knowing nothing is guaranteed and believing you made the right choice for you.

Are You Making a Difference?

How do you define success? We all want it. We all work hard to get it, but how do you define it? Success is something everyone chases—we desire it, and we live for the day we achieve it. For so many, it is the way they define their lives. For many, success means money, fame and fortune, power, the big house, the exotic car, or the beach house. People are consumed trying to obtain the material items of perceived success. When they fail at acquiring the perceived material items of success, they become poisoned with envy of those who already have it. Those who do not obtain the material items of success often experience mental breakdowns, midlife crises, or live unhappily until they make a change or take their last breath.

There are people who tend to define success by the financial fortune of others. With money, you can buy anything you want to help define yourself as being successful. The truth is, money does not equate to success. Money enables you to buy lots of stuff, but it will never bring you complete and total happiness. It will only enable you to purchase more items. For me, success means supporting my family by spending time with them, enjoying the work I do, and living with a purpose. For some, it means contributing to a cause that they believe in; and for others, it is defined by their ability to make things happen for themselves and for others. Or it is the sense of joy one gains when their finished work brings happiness to others. If your work doesn't add to your sense of happiness and joy, then no matter how much money you earn or awards you receive, you will never truly feel or believe you have achieved success.

Many people believe that success is defined by the sense of balance in their lives. They believe success is only truly achieved when their life is no longer living in chaos and a sense of peace has been achieved. They believe that work is not all about achieving success, and it needs to be balanced with other aspects in their lives. When your work totally consumes you and leaves no time for family, physical exercise, relationships, or time for spiritual growth, your life is out of balance and is not successful. An unbalanced life can lead to illness, family turmoil, and failure as the missing true value your life has to offer will be lost.

One of the ways I define success is to ask myself, "Am I making a difference?" How will my life be summed when my eulogy is presented at my funeral? Will people be talking about how much money I made, will they be saying, "Good riddance," or will they be talking about the contributions I made in the lives of others? Will they say how blessed they were to have known me as a friend, a husband, father, an uncle, a son, a brother, or a coworker? I believe a person's success is ultimately defined by the good they do, by the contributions they make into other people's lives, and the positive difference they have made in others.

So many people believe that you are not successful unless you win. This belief robs you and keeps you from giving yourself enough credit. I have found time and again that losing can be more of a success than winning. Many of us miss the point that success does not lie in the results of MONEY, FAME, and FORTUNE. Success lies in the progress we make in our lives. Did we make a difference?

Yes, we all want to be successful. The issue with this is we believe the only way to get what we want is by being successful through MONEY, FAME, and FORTUNE. The easiest way to understand this is if you were to lose everything you own, will you be defined by what you had or defined by your success? If all your perks and money were taken away, would it mean that you have lost your success? Yes, if you believe that success is only defined through the accumulation of material items. No, if you believe that your success is defined by the difference you have made in the world.

So, what is the correct way to define success? I believe it depends on the individual. Success is only important inasmuch as what the meaning holds for us as individuals. Your idea of success will differ from my idea of success. The way you define success lies within your purpose. Why do you want success? When you can answer this question, you will discover the definition of what success really means to you.

Possibilities

Have you ever thought, "Man, if I just had [insert item here], I will be successful!"? That one thing that would give you the competitive edge you need to win big just one time. What if I told you that you already have that one thing you are seeking? Would you believe me?

I am pretty sure that some of you would think that I am crazy, or perhaps you already know that. But there have been many businesspeople, athletes, students, and veterans who I have worked closely with who thought the same thing when we first began working together.

There is no place on any team for individuals who are not mentally tough enough to deal with difficult situations that can arise unexpectedly. The ones who complete the mission or close the tough deals are the ones who keep moving forward as others drop out and quit. There is an excellent book on this called *Extreme Ownership: How US Navy SEALs Lead and Win* by Jocko Willink and Leif Babin. In the book, they discuss how, if we want to be successful in all aspects of life, we must own every action and decision we make.

Stop Taking Criticism So Personally

Be kind, for everyone you meet is fighting a harder battle.

—Plato

How do you feel when someone criticizes you? If you are like most people, your reaction and response depend on many factors. It may depend on who is criticizing you. Your mood that day and disposition can also play an important role. Of course, it can also depend on how they criticize you. Regardless of the situation, you can change your reaction to the criticism. You can learn to control your emotional reaction to criticism and not let it impact your self-esteem.

When you are receiving criticism, it is important to consider the source. Someone you do not know posting a comment about you online is much different than hearing something negative from someone close to you. The messenger of the criticism is important. Another consideration is the motivation for their criticism. Are they trying to help or hurt? Is the criticism constructive or destructive? Understanding the source of the criticism can help you grow professionally or tear you down internally.

If the feedback is coming from someone who is trying to help, then take time to focus on what you can gain from their words. For example, a football player who is told by his coach that he needs to do better at knowing his role during each play can take that information and improve by studying his playbook. They can become a student of the game. There is power in listening to criticism.

What other people think about your skills, characteristics, and knowledge has no impact on who you are as a person. Their opinion is not your reality, it is theirs. Just because you think someone is cruel does not make them cruel. Detach from the feedback and remember that it does not define you. You define you. Feedback and criticism can be difficult to take under any circumstances. Remember who you are and learn from the feedback that is provided. Remember to pay attention to the person delivering the criticism and how you can channel it to improve yourself in a positive way. How much does their opinion really matter to you?

A Word about Your Online Relationships

Surround yourself with only people who are going to lift you higher.
—Oprah Winfrey

We ALL do it. We are so busy and pressured to get everything done that we dash off an email without reading it through or checking the spelling and grammar. Or we make a comment or a joke that we think is a joke in an email or on social media networks only to find at the end of our day that we have been fired. The young lady who made a racist tweet discovered at her expense that anything you say can and will be repeated or passed around online.

One of the key issues with using email is the lack of "tone" that you receive when speaking to someone in person. It lacks the human touch. If you work in a cubicle-based office where the people on your team are sitting next to you but you use email to communicate, you can expect a breakdown in communication. Email is impersonal and does nothing to improve relationships. If what you need to discuss is something important that includes others outside of the office, then use email. Or speak with the individual and then follow up to confirm your understanding of the discussion via email. A good practice before sending an email is to take the time to double-check what you are sending to be sure you are as clear as possible and that it is error-free.

Something to consider when sending work through email is to never send a message that you would be embarrassed to see posted online. Always be careful with what you share in email. One CEO made the mistake of emailing an employee he trusted that he would be offline for a couple of days to deal with some personal issues. When he returned, his "trusted employee" had stolen valuable assets, and a larger company was looking to purchase his business in a hostile takeover bid.

Social media and online discussions can spread like wildfire. Only contribute the bare minimum and never post personal information that might be used against you. If you feel you have something helpful to say to others, join the discussion. Do not use social media as your soapbox to spout your own views and controversial opinions that will lead to a destructive conversation. If you want to advance your career as an expert in your industry, don't try to boast about your skills and accomplishments. Stay humble! Your expertise will speak for itself when you post intelligent responses and remarks.

Most importantly, never "troll" anyone on a social media platform, and do not respond if you are the one being "trolled." When you demote yourself to their level, you become equal to their negativity. Ultimately, this will affect your mind-set, and the best thing to do is to ignore it. If you cannot ignore the troll, understand that everyone is entitled to their own opinion and respond accordingly. Remember, our relationships are as much about what we do as what we do not do. Be courteous and polite to others and see what a difference it can make to all your relationships.

Stop Being Sick and Tired of Not Knowing What You Want from Life

Young men, be careful what you want, for you will surely get it.
—Ralph Waldo Emerson addressed a
graduating class at Harvard University

Every year thousands of kids are asked what they want to be when they grow up. Many do not know and remain undecided through the course of their first few years of college. Even worse, many adults are still struggling to discover what they want from life. Like many, they fall into the trap of doing what is expected of them. The mediocrity of continuous repetition sinks in. They find themselves bored, unsatisfied, and continuously making poor decisions based on the life they are now living. They never follow the dreams they had as a kid; instead, they wander aimlessly without any goals or direction.

That, to me, is terrifying.

If you do not know what you want in life, it is time for you to figure it out. People who know what they want function better in society and have more to provide. They know where they are headed, are happier individuals, and make better life decisions.

7 TIPS to help you DISCOVER what you want in LIFE.

1. Be selfish with your time. If you are constantly saying yes to others, your time will be wasted. Time needed for important commitments will be lost, and there will be no time left for you to figure out what you want from life. Put yourself at the top of your priority list. Ask yourself what you would be doing right now if you had no family, friends, or job obligations.

2. Live without regrets. You cannot change the past so don't focus on changing it. Learn from your mistakes and move forward. It is your life, and you should live it the way you want that makes you happy. Constantly regretting the past prevents you from growing into the person you want to be in the future.

3. Sit down and really think about what you need most in your life. Is it family and love? The freedom of creative expression? Financial security or serving others? List your priorities. Think about the legacy you want to leave when you exit this world.

4. Find what makes you happy. Is it being around kids or helping the elderly? Maybe it is traveling or owning a successful business. Determine the one thing that brings joy to your world and surround yourself with it.

5. Know what upsets you. Be specific. If you do not like your office job, figure out what exactly you do not like about it. Is it your workload? Or your freeloading coworkers? Or maybe it is being inside when you would rather be outside all day long. Can you fix it or make the necessary changes to stop what upsets you?

6. Remain positive. It may take time to find what you're passionate about. You are likely to have some detours along the way and make some decisions that will affect how you

continue. Keeping a positive attitude will help you stay pointed in the right direction.

7. Ask questions. Are some of your thoughts limiting beliefs? Things like "I'm not smart enough to do that" or "Artists have to starve before hitting it big" are thoughts that limit you from taking the action to explore whether this is something you might be interested in doing.

Not knowing what you want to do with your life can be frustrating, depressing, and, many times, terrifying. We all have a purpose, but many have not been successful in discovering theirs. Not knowing where you are going can lead you to making poor choices along the way as well.

Anyone Can Realize Success

Growing up, my parents, grandparents, aunts and uncles all told me, "When you grow up, you can be whatever you want to be." I believed what they told me, and for the most part, it has come true. But I also realize that it has not come true for many others. As a young person, only my imagination limited my ideas of what I dreamed of becoming. I never considered my economic status let alone know what economic status was; it was not until many years later as a young adult did I understand the impact of economic status.

I was taught to believe that if I worked hard, no matter what obstacles were in my way, I would achieve my dreams. To understand the idea of work and economics, you must begin by examining your own reality, whether it was poor or privileged. You must realize that your economic status in society is not solely determined by how hard you work but also social and economic factors such as equal opportunity, education, emotional disposition, and your physical health can play a detrimental role. Most importantly, your level of success will be determined by your level of determination to achieve more.

The growth of the information age and advances in communication technologies has changed the way people learn, work, live, and play. Many senior individuals have been left behind because of the explosive growth in technology. Many people believe they work very hard but are underpaid for their effort. It is the large corporations and world governments that set the terms of trade locally and globally. Many factory workers and field laborers are exploited, producing products that sell for large profits while they are paid minimum wage. These same conglomerate corporations and nations make the money while the worker struggles to pay the water bill and roof over their head. This seems to hold true for those in the lower stratifications of society. Once stranded in a job, it becomes an addictive drug needed to gain its fix. You need to keep working even for minimum wage to gain the essentials you need to survive.

Speaking from personal experience, hard work does pay off. It also takes the right opportunities and the ability to take advantage of those opportunities as they come your way. Certainly, it helps to be educated, but education is not a prerequisite to achieve great success. In the early 1970s, Bill Gates dropped out of Harvard. He was unemployed, talking to anyone he could asking for money to fund his idea for a new business. As we all know, the rest is history.

For most people, nothing worth doing comes easy. It takes determination and a strong work ethic to be successful. However, even though everything is done correctly, with determination and a strong work ethic, there will be failures that stem from economic factors. Consider the rise in the cost of petroleum-based fuels. With the rise in fuel costs, most businesses and every individual in the world has been affected. Many workers are suffering from the rising cost in essentials needed to survive while still unemployed from the 2008 economic recession. Other workers stared the possibility of being laid off in the eye as the perceived downward trend continued. The automobile industry was brought to its knees, unable to sell the products that just a few years back were their best sellers, requiring the industry to redefine itself. As a result, workers lost their jobs. To this day, many workers have not recovered.

Take what you are dealt in life and make the best of it. You have choices. What you make of your choices is what counts most. I have worked since I was ten years old, and for more than fifty-one years, I have never been unemployed. Have I been lucky? Maybe! I work to pay bills and buy the things I want, but I also work because it provides satisfaction. I enjoy the feeling of accomplishment and being a part of something bigger than myself. Today, I work at the things that interest me most, but my family remains the reason of every endeavor. Even when you own your own company, you must strive for a balance between achieving personal gain, your personal life, and your company's success.

Don't use economic status, education, or the lack of luck as excuses for not achieving your success. Anyone can realize success, but it depends on how hard you want to work for it. It depends on your level of determination to make it happen. Take the first step toward your success by deciding that you deserve better. Let nothing stand in your way as you work to make your success happen.

Appreciate Life

Appreciation is a wonderful thing. It makes what is excellent in others belong to us as well.

—Voltaire

Have you ever struggled to find the answer to "What do I have to be grateful for?" I know there have been times when I was stumped, and I am certain you have experienced the same. When was the last time you stopped to consider the everyday things you take for granted and underappreciate? Do you hear more complaining and blaming or more praise for what you have in your life? Do you spread thanks, cheer, and good will, or do you contribute to your own doom and demise? Even though life seems like it is a constant uphill battle, there is much to appreciate about life.

Being grateful is life changing as it lifts your spirit. The problem seems to be that people become unfocused while often thinking about what they do not have rather than the things they do have. When you get stuck in the rut of wanting and needing, you miss being grateful for what you already have. There are times when goals, people, or situations might not measure up to expectations. During these times, it is your expectation that is the problem. Many times, too much focus has been placed on expected results rather than appreciation. By not placing value on what is important, you allow others or materialistic items to take over your life.

How many times have you heard "The grass is not always greener on the other side" or "I didn't realize what I had until it was gone"? Many times, it was not the things you owned or the things you considered important; rather, it was what you missed along the way that has been lost. Setting your sights on wanting and needing blurs your vision of the world around you. When you appreciate and are grateful for what you have, you understand what will be missed when it is gone. Family and loved ones should always be appreciated and cherished. Let the people around you know every day how much you appreciate them and how important they are to you. You just never know when they will be gone from this world.

We all have been given precious gifts, and many of us have failed to recognize them. By noticing that everyday ordinary things like the birds singing, the butterfly on a flower, the sunrise and sunset, the gentle breeze on a hot day, fresh snow, parents, children, and grandchildren, it becomes easy to see how blessed we truly are. Taking a closer look will reveal that the grass is not always greener on the other side. When you begin to appreciate the simple gifts that life has already provided you, you will live a fuller life. Be grateful for the things you have and the gifts the world has given you. Certainly, there will be days that you struggle, but all you must do is take a closer look at the world around you. Realizing what you already have will help you appreciate life for what it is.

About the Author

Jeff Heiser is a motivational speaker, author, podcaster, and United States Navy veteran. He has made it his personal life mission to teach others to think differently about their life, work, and goals. Through his work, he shares his belief that anything is possible with the right mind-set. Jeff is an accomplished motivator, leader and communicator that has helped many individuals change their lives by changing the way they think.

His diverse background has enabled him to help others change their lives by helping them to think differently and to overcome imaginary internal mental boundaries. Jeff has coached and mentored business leaders, military personnel, young adults, students, and aspiring athletes, enabling them to take their game to the next level. He is an expert in how one can change their life by tapping into their full human potential.

As a speaker and expert in achieving the mind-set needed to bring change to one's life, Jeff has addressed audiences across the United States. His audiences have included admirals, generals, university presidents, top business leaders, elite athletes and students. His unique perspective on what it takes to succeed has helped countless individuals reach their full potential for success.

To learn more about Jeff Heiser or to book Jeff as a guest speaker, check out his website at https://www.JeffreyHeiser.com

CPSIA information can be obtained
at www.ICGtesting.com
Printed in the USA
BVHW072009120819
555662BV00006B/832/P